Dedication

Raylan:

You are stronger and more resilient than I have ever imagined you would be. You have overcome so many obstacles in your life, and I can't wait to see the man you become.

Amber:

You are the love of my life, and I am glad you finally took me up on my offer to get coffee on that Sunday afternoon.

DIGITAL MARKETING for RURAL SMALL BUSINESSES

★ ★ ★ ★ ★

A Comprehensive Guide To Getting Found on the Internet

Chad J. Treadway

Digital Marketing for Rural Small Businesses: A Comprehensive Guide to Getting Found on the Internet

Copyright © 2023 by Chad J. Treadway

Published by Cube Creative Design Publishing (Asheville, NC)

Book cover by Joe Masterson and Chad J. Treadway

First edition, September 2023

ISBN: 979-8-98852-891-3

Library of Congress Control Number: 2023915281

Created in the United States of America

Learn more about Chad J. Treadway visit RuralDigitalMarketing.com or visit CubeCreative.Design. Special discounts are available on quantity book purchases. Contact Chad@RuralDigitalMarketing.com for information.

Contents

Read This First

If you are reading this, that means you are like me and also read the introductions. Kudos to you!

WHO THIS BOOK IS FOR

Every time I thought about it, a modified song lyric always came to mind: It's for all the lovers, all the haters, and all the people that work for or own a rural small business.

HOW IT'S LAID OUT

As I started thinking about the concept of the book, I was reminded of a quote by Zig *Ziglar* from his book, Selling 101; in it, he says that "Those of you who read the Bible know (and whether you are a believer or not most people respect the fact) that Christ was a powerful persuader. I encourage you to go to a good bookstore, buy a red-letter edition of the Bible (because the words of Christ are printed in red), and read. You will make an amazing discovery, namely, that when people asked Christ a question, He either responded with a question or a parable—both of which are tools for persuasion."

Needless to say, the idea of explaining the concept through a story spoke to me. Therefore, the book is one part fiction and one part nonfiction. In other words, you can't put this book in a corner.

WHY WRITE THE BOOK

In all seriousness, the book stems from several things. Firstly, I was having a conversation with my business partner about travel to and fro each day. He remarked that he averages about five to ten miles a day. I looked at him and said, "Dude, I have already driven 20 miles before 8:00 just taking my son to school."

The second epiphany was realizing how Google and the other search engines only want to show results within a few miles of you. You and I both know windshield time is part of the price we pay to live in a rural area, but the programmers and gurus working on the search engines don't understand that.

The third and final part was that after reading and absorbing all this knowledge, I needed to do something else with it. Blame being the son of a teacher, married to a teacher, and having taught myself for a short while. I felt the need to share with my fellow rural small businesses how to do what I do. Thus, the book started to come to fruition.

OTHER NOTABLES

As you read, you will undoubtedly pick up on the puns, dad jokes, movie quotes (or loose interpretations of them), as well as bands, song titles, and song lyrics. I apologize now, as that is how my brain works, as evidenced by this introduction.

Secondly, I have made every effort to thoroughly reference and cite my sources. I'm sure other books, articles, and podcasts have influenced the concepts, techniques, and information that aren't mentioned. Check out the website (RuralDigitalMarketing.com/resources) for an up-to-date list of places where you can find information if you are looking to dive deeper into Digital Marketing for Rural Small Businesses.

Lastly, in the sense of transparency and accountability, I wanted to tell you, dear reader, that 4.22% of any commissions made on the sale of this goes directly to one of the various charities helping to fund research and to help support those who have Type 1 (Juvenile)

Diabetes. You may ask yourself why 4.22% and why those particular non-profits. The simple answer is my son (Raylan) was diagnosed on April 22 (4/22) with Type 1. The Type 1 Diabetes (T1D) community and the T1D non-profits have helped us immensely with support and knowledge since his diagnosis. This small donation is my way of giving back and helping to find a cure.

1 | Walk This Way

When you hear something, you will forget it.
When you see something, you will remember it.
But not until you do something, will you understand it.

— Old Chinese Proverb

Success is on the other side of "You can't do this."

— James Altucher

It was a day much like any other day. Well, I guess I should say it was what had become the new normal day. Business had slowed, and I don't mean the ebbs and flows or cycle of busy and slow times. I mean, it was *slow.* Honestly, I wasn't sure I could make a go of the business any longer.

I had left work and was driving down the road with a million things on my mind. Mainly, how was I going to keep the business afloat? I remember stopping at the red light at the busiest intersection in town. As the light changed, I gunned it, ready to run my errands and get home.

I got about halfway through the intersection and saw a car blasting through on the left. I knew I couldn't stop, so I swerved to the right. Then as if in slow motion, I heard the screamin' tires, the bustin' glass.

The next thing I know, I'm standing in the middle of a strange digital city. It feels a little like my small town, but at the same time, it is vastly different. As I look around, it looks like a cross between something out of Star Wars and what people think the cities of tomorrow will look like.

As I walk down the street, I keep looking around, and I can see these thin wisps of lights running every which way, and I can hear faint conversations, songs, and scenes from TV shows and movies playing. I walk up to one of the businesses and look in one of the shop windows. I can't see in the shop at all. It looks more like a digital screen. I can barely make out what appears to be someone scrolling down a page of a website, pausing to read, then quickly scrolling again.

I begin to wonder what this is. Then it hits me. I have no clue how I got here or, for that matter, where here is!

I wander around a bit more, trying to come to grips with where "here" is. As I round a corner, I realize that I'm not alone as there are people from all walks of life wandering around. Some are dressed in business suits and look like they belong on the streets of New York City, and others look more like me, simple hard-working folk. I tried to stop one of the suits, but he acted as if I wasn't even there. I reached out to another and another and kept getting the brush-off. Frustrated, I walked over and sat down on a bench beside a gentleman.

I murmured to what I thought was myself, "What is this place?"

The man on the bench looks at me and says, "Welcome to the jungle."

"The jungle?"

He replied, "Yep, welcome to the jungle. You're gonna' die," in his best Axl Rose impression, and then burst out laughing.

I looked at him with curiosity.

"Just kidding. I tend to quote random song lyrics, movie quotes, bad puns, and even worse, dad jokes. My name is Viator." He pronounced it like 'Weatore' and stuck out his hand to shake mine.

I introduced myself back, shook his hand. "Where am I really?"

"You *are* in the jungle, but not the jungle you might be thinking of. This is the online business jungle. You see all these people—they all own a business or are in sales or marketing."

He pointed to a guy and referred to him as the "mad man" because he worked for a major marketing firm in NYC on Madison Avenue.

"He won't ever talk to you because you're a small business, and he only wants to go after the enterprise-size businesses. Then you have the lady over there who owns a hair salon. The guy next to her owns a plumbing company." He continued, pointing out several people, both "mad men" types and people like me.

I was astonished at the wide variety of businesses represented around us. "How do you know so much about these people?"

He looked at me and smiled. "I know them because I have been here a while. You see, I was able to help many of the small businesses here at some point to navigate the jungle. It's what I do. I help small businesses grow, especially those in rural markets."

"What do you mean to grow?"

"I help people grow their business using the power of the Internet. Reach into your pocket and pull out your phone. You have the power of the Internet right there. You are mere seconds away from the great curiosity engine, Google. You can Google anything you can imagine. People all over the world search for anything and everything, and I help small businesses show up for those searches. Try it yourself."

Pulling out my phone, I typed in "Google" and saw a thin wisp of light travel from my phone; within less than a second, the Google search bar appeared in the air in front of me. I typed in stuff about my business and watched the same light appear again.

I looked at Viator and asked, "Are we *in* the Internet?"

He shook his head. "No, you are just seeing a visualization of it."

I sat there looking around, amazed by everything and still trying to take it all in.

Viator broke the silence that stretched between us. "You live in a rural area, don't you?"

I nodded.

"I bet you probably think you can't harness what you see around you. But I'm here to tell you that you can—if you know how."

It was like he was reading my mind. "Okay, tell me this: say I wanted to grow my business like you say you help people do. How would I go about it?"

Viator grinned. "I'm glad you asked. In his book *Traction*, Gino Wickman said it best: 'You have to be willing to be open to new and different ideas. If you don't know something, you have to admit that you don't know. You have to be willing to ask for and receive help. Most of all, you have to know your strengths and weaknesses and let other people who are more skilled than you in a certain area take charge.'[1]

"In other words," he said, "think of it as these three steps."

> **Step 1**: Specifically ask for help.

> **Step 2**: See that what you have been doing might not be the best solution for your business. It's not to say what you have done is wrong or you shouldn't be doing something. You might just need to focus your efforts elsewhere.

> **Step 3**: Be vulnerable, open-minded, and growth-oriented.

I thought for a moment and agreed with what he said. I then went on to explain to him the situation I was in.

Having listened to my plight, Viator stood and extended a hand down to me. "Are you ready to grow your business and get out of the jungle?"

I took his hand and stood. "Most definitely. Which way do we go?"

"A journey of a thousand miles starts with a single step. Are you sure you are ready and willing?"

My excitement building, I nodded. "Yes, let's go!"

"Then I will help guide you on this journey, but you must take the first step, and that step is to ask."

"Ask?"

"Yes."

"I just told you that I was ready," I said in a frustrated voice.

He began to lower himself back onto the bench. "You said you were ready, but you have yet to ask. Asking is the first step."

I thought for a moment and wondered, did I not ask? I told him I was ready, but then it hit me. I never said I wanted him to help me specifically. I said, "Please, will you help me?"

"My pleasure," he said as he stood again.

I looked down the street and saw many people headed down the main road. I looked around and saw a few headed down a side road. I thought surely we would go down the main road and started walking down it.

Viator looked at me and gestured for me to follow him. "That's not the way! You need to *Walk This Way.*" The Aerosmith song started playing in the background. Was this really what it would be like? Would my random thoughts trigger something?

Either way, I looked at Viator as he took about five steps, and his right arm went up and formed a V then his hand was straight. He then placed his left arm behind him in a similar fashion. He began to pump his arms to and fro, which looked like the paintings in ancient Egypt. After about ten steps like this, he looked back and said, "You're not walking like an Egyptian! I told you to walk this way, and if I walk like an Egyptian and start singing the song, you had better do it too!"

"I don't see how this will help the business. It just makes us look like idiots!" I protested, refusing to make a fool of myself.

He looked back and dropped his pose. "You are not ready, then. If you are unwilling to try and experiment, I can't help you." With a disappointed air, he returned to his seat on the bench.

As I stood there dumbfounded, I knew I had to get out of here and back home to the business—and, more importantly, to my family and friends.

I tried Googling how to get out of the jungle—the digital jungle, that is—and get out of the Internet, but I couldn't find any results. After a while of fruitless searching I gave up and sat on the ground. I looked up as Viator's shoes came into view.

"Are you done?" he asked.

"What do you mean, done?"

"Are you ready to go and grow?"

I stared hopelessly at the dead-end results of my Google searching. "I'm ready to get out of here, I know that much."

"That's not what I asked. Are you ready to stop wondering if the business can make it? Are you ready to stop wasting time and money on efforts that get you little or no return? Are you ready to see the business grow?!"

I stood; Viator's questions had begun to light a fire under me and chase away my hopelessness. "Yes, I think I am!"

He looked at me and raised an eyebrow. "You know what you have to do, right?"

"Walk like an Egyptian?"

"Yes!" He said, elated, and struck the pose while walking.

I did the same, following him for twenty paces. Viator stopped when he looked back at me. "Okay, that's enough silliness."

"What?"

"I just wanted to see if you would do it," he said with a laugh.

Walking down the main strip, we turned down the road I had seen a few take before. As I looked down the road, it appeared to get rougher and rougher. I wondered if we were headed for the seedy dark side of town. I looked at Viator, concerned. "Are you crazy? That can't be the right way!"

"Again, here you go questioning me. If I am to help you, I have to show you the good, the bad, and the ugly.

"You have to trust me. I have taken many businesses down this path, it's not easy, and there will be times you'll question if this will work. It's not an overnight success or a magic bullet. However, those who stick with it have been rewarded handsomely. The old main road we just left will only lead to failure, as you will eventually see. "

I looked at him and shrugged. "Well, what do I have to lose?"

And so our journey began.

FAILURE VERSUS PROSPERITY

As we walked down the road, Viator explained that many small businesses fail. Fundera looked at the Bureau of Labor Statistics and found that approximately two out of ten small businesses fail within the first year and nearly four out of ten fail by the end of the second year. Furthermore, 50 to 90% of small businesses won't make it past the five-year mark.[2]

Small businesses also typically fail to grow past the point where the owner(s) can make a comfortable living. Unfortunately, they either give up hope that their business can be anything more than a low-paying, self-created job, or they accept this as their fate.

Viator reached into his laptop bag, pulled out a notepad and pen, and handed them to me.

I took it from his hand and asked. "What is this for?"

He said, "You might find it helpful to take some notes so you can remember everything better."

Viator then gave me two examples: "Captain Nemo's Nautilus Nautical Tours" and "Chaz's Charters." Nemo was working 12-16 hours a day, six and seven days a week. The problem was he was always running payday to payday, and never getting ahead. Then on the flip side, you had Chaz's Charters, who had five boats, and 18 people dedicated to keeping the people on the fish.

The difference between the two is that Chaz realized that even though his passion was fishing and being a captain, he needed to work "on" the business and not "in" the business if he was to be successful.

YOU HAVE TO SPEND MONEY TO MAKE MONEY

"I know you have heard the old saying you have to spend money to make money."

I nodded. "Yes, I get it. But what do you do when you don't have it to begin with?"

He looked at me and, without missing a beat, said, "You're missing the point. You can either spend time trying to save a dollar or spend a dollar and get your time back.

"Think about this: In 2016, Netflix introduced the 'Skip Intro' button. Think about how often you have used it to skip over the recap and opening credits. While this might not seem like a huge deal, it bought you and Netflix's members time. According to them, as of March 17, 2022, the 'Skip Intro' button had been 'pressed 136 million times, saving members an astonishing 195 years in cumulative time!'[3] The bottom line is, if you can spend a few dollars to save time, you should—because time is one thing you can never buy back."

WHEN TIMES ARE TOUGH, MAINTAIN OR INCREASE YOUR INVESTMENTS

I sidestepped a pothole in the road and peered at Viator skeptically. "I get what you're saying, but what do I do when times are hard? I mean, it's hard enough to spend money to make money, then you combine it with tough economic times. What would I do then?"

Viator asked me if I had ever heard of a study by Roland Vaile and Reavis Cox that came out in a 1927 Harvard Business Review. And, of course, I said no, thinking only this guy would quote some article from a hundred years ago.

He winked. "I didn't expect you to, so I'll give you the 'too long and didn't read (tl;dr;) synopsis.

"Think about this: during the United States Great Recession of 1920 and 1921, Vaile and Cox discovered that companies that continued to invest in advertising drove higher sales and growth than their competitors. They did this by dividing and comparing the performances of three different groups of companies: those that didn't advertise, those that cut advertising, and businesses that invested extra in advertising.

"They found sales and growth for companies that invested in advertising grew visibly during the recession, but this also continued to grow afterward. In comparison, the businesses that had cut advertising continued to see a decline up to three years after the recession ended."[4]

Taking my silence for confusion, he explained, "During The Great Recession, more research was conducted on how companies handled their budgets. This revealed that businesses that had cut their marketing budgets initially fared better during the recession but experienced negative performances after it ended. Here again, companies that started or increased their marketing were shown to have performed better post-recession and experienced an average growth in market share of 1.3%."[5]

"So, what you are saying is that when times get hard, I have to pump even more money into my marketing and advertising?" I asked.

"Yes! I know it's hard, but I have seen it work, and as I have just explained, we have historical proof! If you are going to be successful, you have to keep targeting your prospects and market to your existing clientele."

YOU HAVE TO KNOW THE FACTS

We were still walking down the road when we came to a medical facility, and Viator started to walk in the lobby. I will admit, I was puzzled about why he would be walking in. Was he somehow hurt or in pain, and I didn't know it?

Almost as fast as the thought had formed in my mind, Viator looked over and said, "You're wondering what this has to do with growing your business, right?"

The look on my face must have been of shock and disbelief, as he laughed and turned to me. "Your face says it all. Let me explain."

He began by telling a story he had read in Simon Sinek's bestselling book, *Start with Why*. The story goes like this:

> On a cold January day, a 43-old man was sworn in as the chief executive of his country. By his side stood his predecessor, a famous general who, fifteen years earlier, had commanded his nation's armed forces in a war that resulted in the defeat of Germany. The young leader was raised in the Roman Catholic faith. He spent the next five hours watching parades in his honor and stayed up celebrating until three o'clock in the morning.[6]

"Who do you think that was?"

I thought for a moment and answered confidently. "John F. Kennedy."

"Wrong," he shouted.

"What! It has to be JFK," I said.

Viator laughed and shook his head. "You see, Sinek left out an important detail in that story, the date is January 30, 1933, and he was describing Adolf Hitler.

"Think about it like this: if the medical professionals in this facility don't have all the facts, it's hard for them to know how to treat a patient. The same can be said about you and your business; if you and I don't have enough facts, then we can make an educated guess, but we could be drastically wrong."

He brought his hands together with a clap. "This brings me to another point. Do you know your why?"

"My 'why'?"

"Yes. Why do you do what you do?"

I shrugged, plopping into a lobby chair. "Well, I guess to make a living and provide for my family and myself."

Viator sat beside me and shook his head. "That is the easy answer. The money is the result. I mean, what is your real reason? Why do you do what you do? I ask this because it's harder for people to buy from you and your business before you know *why* you're doing it in the first place."

We sat in silence for a bit as I pondered his question. After a time, Viator broke the silence. "I know you are thinking about your 'why.' I can see the wheels turning in your mind. Would you like to know *my* 'why'?"

"Yes!" I exclaimed.

"Before I started helping small businesses like yours, I was working in education and helping to market a performing arts center and a large music festival associated with the institution. At first, I loved what I did. I poured my heart and soul into it. Then things started to change. New management came in, and I realized their 'why' and mine didn't align. It took me several years later to realize that was what happened.

"When I left, I found a new mission and a new passion, and that was helping rural small businesses. My 'why,' or mission, is to help them grow their business. I get excited when they tell me they were able to grow and do something other than work '*in* the business but rather *on* the business."

THE CUSTOMER
ISN'T ALWAYS RIGHT

Viator stood and motioned for me to follow him out of the medical facility. "As we continue on this journey, I also want to tell you that you aren't always going to be right. And when you're wrong, I will tell you, but in a nice way."

"But wait," I protested, pausing in the doorway. "I thought the customer was always right?"

He shook his head, a serious expression on his face. "If someone is being abusive to you or your staff, are they in the right? Their claim might be legitimate, but that doesn't give them the right to bless your staff out."

He went on to tell me about Southwest Airlines. They are known for being customer service-oriented, but in their model, the customer is not always right; the employee is. If a customer treats a Southwest employee rudely or doesn't like the service they offer, the customer is asked to take their business elsewhere.

Viator quoted Sinek again, saying, "It's a subtle irony that one of the best customer service companies in the country focuses on its employees before its customers."[7]

With my head spinning from everything I had just heard and witnessed, we walked back onto the street.

2 | You Have to Know Where You've Been to Know Where You Are Going

Half the money I spend on advertising is wasted; the trouble is, I don't know which half.

— John Wanamaker

If you cannot risk, you cannot grow. If you cannot grow, you cannot become your best. If you cannot become your best, you cannot be happy. If you cannot be happy, what else matters?

— Dr. David Viscott

We walked silently down the road, passing buildings. I couldn't help but think how much it looked like my little downtown mixed with the futuristic structures. I could still see windows, but they were more like screens, and I looked out into the real world through the backside of the Internet. As I looked around, I found myself questioning my decisions. Did I make the right choice? Will Viator help me? I wouldn't dare tell him what I was thinking for fear of yet another tongue-lashing. All I knew was that I owed it to myself to at least see this through.

As we stepped onto the sidewalk, we came across this massive architectural marvel. The cornerstone and the inscription on it declared that it was built the same year my hometown was formed.

Viator broke the contemplative silence that had fallen between us. "Before we continue any further, we must look at where we have been to understand where we need to go."

He then motioned for me to follow him up a broad set of granite steps set into the face of the marvelous structure. Every so often, we came to a small landing, but Viator never seemed to need to catch his breath. Walking up, I could feel that each step was slightly uneven, worn by time and by the footsteps of countless visitors.

As we got to the top landing, we could see the grand marble columns that flanked the entrance. The bottom of the columns were broad, smooth, and polished to perfection. The columns narrowed as they reached toward the sky, and each had intricate flutes that gave way to more delicate carvings.

Inside, it was massive. It looked like a cross between a museum and a library, like something one would see on TV and in movies. The library's high ceilings give it an air of spaciousness, but much of the light was blocked by aisles of towering wooden shelves worn with age and time. Neat rows of study tables occupied the floor, each attended by well-worn chairs and topped with small, emerald-shaded reading lamps that provided a soft, warm glow.

The walls were lined from floor to ceiling with an endless expanse of bookshelves that stretched with the building beyond the limit of my sight. Viator and I walked for what felt like miles down the length of the library, and I looked up and down each aisle, noticing that each had a ladder that rolled along the shelves. We finally came to a section entitled "The History of Sales, Marketing, and Advertising."

This section was filled with books of all shapes and sizes, their spines displaying a multitude of colors, titles, and authors. Viator walked down the aisle, pulled a couple of books from the shelves, and handed them to me. He then scurried up the ladder, pulled a couple more, and pushed off, rolling down the aisle and pulling another and another. This went on until I couldn't hold much more.

He scanned the stack of titles in my arms and gave a satisfied nod. "That should do. Let's sit down over there—" He pointed to one of the tables. "—and I can explain why we are here and what these have to do with online marketing."

I gratefully followed him to a nearby table and released my burden with a *thud*.

Taking a seat across the table from me, Viator folded his hands in front of him and leaned forward. "You see, we have to know where we have been to understand where we are going. Take this book, for example, which is full of newspaper and magazine ads. In their golden age, this is where you needed to be to reach your clientele."

He opened another, and a small screen popped up with speakers. It started playing radio ads and jingles. Yet another was opened, and a small screen with TV ads from my childhood started showing.

He then pulled one of the thickest books from the stack, which had to be at least four inches thick. He then pulled on the thinnest books, which was about as thick as a marker lying on its side. He looked at me and asked if I knew what they were, but he didn't wait for me to answer. "These are phonebooks.

"This bigger one is from a long-forgotten time before the internet, where if you needed to find a business, this is where you would look. The thinner one is from more recently; flip through both pages and tell me what you see."

As I thumbed through the pages, I could see ads for businesses like mine in the bigger one, but in the smaller one, there were only one or two of them. "First off, the gray and yellow pages are much smaller in the newer version compared to the older one."

"Exactly! Many people I have met over the years still think these are viable avenues to market their business. I'm not here to say yes or no, but unless it has been tested, you have no way of knowing. Also, in more rural areas, we still have the phone book delivered to us. In most urban areas, you may have to request one specifically, and there have been numerous tries to ban them altogether."

"Banned!?"

"Yep! Way back in 2012, several cities, San Francisco and Seattle being two, tried to ban their publishing and delivery." Viator smirked, then explained, "According to Catherine Rauschuber, when San Francisco wanted to ban the phonebook, *The Yellow Pages* was distributing 'approximately 1.6 million phonebooks' per year. With the average book being 4.33 pounds, it created 'nearly seven million pounds of waste' and cost taxpayers $300 per ton to trash or recycle![1]

"Also, think about how the Washington Utilities and Transportation Commission 'eliminated a requirement that telephone companies must provide a printed White Pages directory.' They then made the companies that wanted to send a physical White Pages directory have an opt-out option.[2]

"Now I ask you, do you think that most of your clientele are looking in here—" He pointed to the newer phonebook. "—to find your business, or are they just going to Google you or look you up on social media?"

I chuckled. "I'm guessing they will do the latter, as I don't know when *I* last picked up a phonebook."

Viator nodded. "For most businesses I have worked with and people I have talked to, they say the same thing. What do you think about newspapers, radio, and TV?"

I looked at him, puzzled. "I don't know. I guess they could work?"

"Yes, they can work." He held up a finger. "But only for the right audience. That means you have to know *where* and *who* your ideal clientele is. I like to think of all advertising as brand awareness, unless you're offering a sale or a discount for services."

I thumbed through the pages of the books Viator had pulled, absorbing what I could but still not knowing exactly what I was looking for. I kept thinking about all the things I had tried in the past. It was always hard to tell what was working and what wasn't.

Viator must have heard the gears turning in my head again because he looked up from the books he was thumbing through and said, "I know you are wondering if what you have done before worked. Think about this: way back before the dawn of the Internet, people such as yourself only had four options for attracting attention:

1. Buying an ad in the newspaper, on the radio, or on TV.
2. Hiring a PR firm or trying to write a press release yourself
    and submitting it to various media outlets in hopes
    they would run it or contact you for a bigger story.
3. Sending direct mailings to people.
4. Hitting the phones and calling people at all times of
    the day or evening and convincing them to buy.

"The problem with all these options is that it was harder to target specific buyers with personalized content. If your brand was large enough, you could still use it to reach buyers, but some of these methods are cost-prohibitive for a small business."

ADVERTISING DEFINED

Viator spread his palms flat on the table. "I want you to picture a small, fast-moving creek running through your area. Now imagine that same creek as your prospect's mind.

"Now with advertising, you can try to put something in the creek, but it's hard to get it to go in. You compound the fact that your offer is at the edge of the creek, where it is somewhat unnoticeable. Therefore, you must put it in the middle of the stream where it can be seen and garner attention."[3]

ADS CAN BE EXPENSIVE

"So you think I need to advertise more?"

Viator shook his head. "No, that isn't what I'm saying at all. Many people I talk to believe that a single ad or a short run of ads will have people beating down their doors wanting to hire them. The problem is that advertising can be extremely expensive."

He pulled a book from the stack and opened it—somewhat magically—to the page he was looking for. "Take a look at this," he said as he handed it to me.

The paragraph read, "It cost $9,000 a minute to fight World War II. It cost $22,000 a minute to fight the Vietnam War. A one-minute commercial on the NFL Super Bowl [in 1992] will cost you $1.5 million."[4]

"Well, of course, the Super Bowl would cost that much; it's par for the course there," I scoffed. "But I'm sure I could run an ad in my local area much cheaper than a Super Bowl commercial."

"That isn't the point of showing you that. The point is, ads are expensive. According to my research for a local television station, if you ran a 30-second commercial, it would average between $100 to $1,500, depending on the time of day. That also doesn't include production of the ad."

I frowned. "Ok, well, what about a billboard? I have friends who have seen great success with those."

"Billboard advertising costs vary according to format, circulation, demographics, and impressions. On average, physical billboards will cost $750 to $1,500 per month in rural areas, $1,500 to $2,000 per month in small-to-midsize towns, and $14,000 or more in major metropolitan areas. And depending on the location, digital billboards might cost more than $15,000."

He continued, "Now I bet you are thinking, 'What about social media ads?' Social media ads average $1.86 per click on Facebook. The bottom line is that you may spend $60 per month or up to $6,000 per month for other ads."

I let out a long whistle. "Wow, that sure is a lot."

Viator spread his hands placatingly. "Now, I'm not saying that paid ads are good or bad; I'm just putting it out there for you to make an informed decision."

MARKETING DEFINED

"Hang on a minute," I interrupted. "There's something bugging me. What's the difference between selling, advertising, and marketing?"

Viator grabbed a book and quickly thumbed to a well-worn page. "Here, look at how Peter Doyle defines marketing in his book *Marketing Management & Strategy*. It reads, 'Marketing is a philosophy of business that places the customer at the center of the universe.'

"In other words, it doesn't matter what business you're in or what part of the business you handle. Marketing needs to be at its core."

He spun the book back around and almost instinctively flipped to another page, then turned it back to me. "Look here."

"Selling tries to push the customer to buy what the business has," read the paragraph under his pointing finger. "Marketing, on the other hand, tries to get the organization to develop and offer what the customer will find is of real value. In this way, marketing seeks to build long-term, mutually beneficial partnerships between the organization and its customers."[5]

As I raised my gaze from the book, Viator grinned. "You see," he said, "if your business is to grow, you have to invest in marketing to promote it."

He then grabbed another book and flipped through the pages as if he were a man possessed. He obviously knew what he was looking for. Once he came to the page he wanted, he ran around the desk to stand at my side, pointing at the page. "Here, look at this definition:

> If the circus is coming to town and you paint a sign saying, "Circus Coming to the Showground Saturday," that's advertising.
>
> If you put the sign on the back of an elephant and walk it into town, that's promotion.
>
> If the elephant walks through the mayor's flower bed and the local newspaper writes a story about it, that's publicity.

And if you get the mayor to laugh about it, that's public relations.

If the town's citizens go to the circus, you show them the many entertainment booths, explain how much fun they'll have spending money at the booths, answer their questions, and, ultimately, they spend a lot at the circus, that's sales.

And if you planned the whole thing, that's marketing."[6]

I chuckled a bit at the thought of the spectacle of that analogy. While it was funny, it also helped clear things up for me.

Then without notice, Viator stiffened and whipped his gaze around the room. Lowering his voice, he said intently, "We need to head out now. They know you're here, and we need to get moving fast!"

"Wait, who knows I'm here? What are you talking about?" I protested.

Viator's face took on a look of determination and scorn. I followed his gaze and saw three people approaching us from the entrance of the library.

The trio exuded a sense of authority and professionalism. They were dressed in black with white shirts and black ties, their unified image projected an unwavering presence. The guys wore pants while the woman wore a black skirt.

At this point I wasn't sure if they were cops or hitmen. Viator looked at me and said, "I don't have time to explain. This is one of those times you need to trust me. Now let's GO!"

We stood and left the books lying on the table. We then crisscrossed the building, moving in and around the shelves like a maze. We then finally made our way to the exit.

I looked at Viator, filling my lungs with fresh air as the library doors closed behind us. "What has you so shaken? Who is this 'they' you're referring to? Who were those people?"

His lips tightened into a grimace. "That was Otto, Constanze, and

Phoebus. I was hoping they wouldn't have caught up to us so soon, but they must have realized you were here and came looking for you."

I must have had a perplexed look on my face because Viator quickly explained that, unlike him, those three were not here to help; they wanted to see me lose in the end. At this point, I was even more confused about who they were and why they were after me.

Viator ran a hand through his hair and exhaled loudly. "I think we have managed to avoid them for the time being, but they will keep coming for you, so we have to move quickly."

With that, he pulled out his phone, tapped it a bit, and the next thing I knew, we were getting into what I could best describe as a car or some sort of vehicle. To be honest, I don't even know how to describe it. Once inside, I presumed there would be a driver or some way to control it, but there wasn't either. This contraption had just two seats and what looked like a digital screen, which Viator tapped on, and then we zoomed away. I didn't know where we were headed; I was just along for the ride.

3 | The Dark Side of Digital Marketing

When people are free to do as they please, they usually imitate one another.

– Eric Hoffer

We sped down the road at a ludicrous speed. As we went, I tried to look out the window to see where we were going, but all I could see were streaks of light. Then almost as suddenly as we started, we came to a screeching halt. The vehicle's doors opened, and Viator climbed out, looked around, and motioned for me to follow.

Looking around, I couldn't help wondering if I hadn't jumped out of the frying pan into the fire. We were in what I would call the rough side of town.

The odd thing was the entire scene was like a melting pot of people. I saw the "Mad Men" and "Mad Women" types in their suits, those who looked like me, and those who might be best described as misfits and drug addicts. Several of the people looked as if they had almost been bled dry. There were several large storefronts. One had a multi-colored sign of red, yellow, green, and blue. One was in shades of blue, and another was in yellowy-orange. All the people in line were taking turns going up to a window, pulling out what looked like loads of money, and walking away with little rectangles or square boxes; some had more than others.

I watched as little wisps of light came out of thin air and looked like they entered the boxes like a needle going into your arm. Some seemed to vanish as quickly as they appeared, and others lingered a bit. Fewer still changed into what looked like money or more information. Many of the people would then take off back down the street we had just walked down, others headed in the opposite direction toward the main road that I had wanted to go down at the start of this thing. At this point, I was really questioning what was going on, especially when we crossed the street and stood in line at the bright multi-colored one.

I couldn't take it any longer, so I nudged Viator and whispered, "What is this, and why are we here?"

"This is the digital marketing district. You see over there is the pay-per-click or PPC line." He pointed to the line under the big blue sign. Then his finger drifted to the other colored signs. "The multicolored one is for social media, and that yellow-orange one is for people who sell products online on the biggest retailer's platform. Let's grab a drink, and I will explain how digital advertising works."

We crossed the street and ducked into a coffee shop called The 9-to-5 Grind. The shop sat on the corner and had an old 50's diner vibe. Truth be told, it might have been and just converted to a coffee shop.

Unlike the chain shops, it didn't have a dark, moody feel. The bar was lined with permanent circular barstools with chrome rings accenting the bubble seats. The counter still had the speckled white and gold flake laminate top. Behind the bar where the kitchen would have been, you could see stacks of beans and coffee roasters with one of the workers attending to it.

The booths were upholstered in the same vibrant vinyl as the barstools and lined the walls. Viator ordered two drinks and led us to a booth in the back. Viator sat with his back to the wall where he could survey the room if Otto, Constanze, and Phoebus were to show up again.

Taking a sip of his drink, Viator said, "I wanted to come here first so you can understand what we will be building to help you grow the business. You see, everything we'll do will start and end with your website. We'll use an ad to help you get a few good leads to start while we build out the rest of your content on your site."

I hummed thoughtfully. "What do you mean by content? I understand what a website is, and we talked about how traditional ads work. What I don't understand is if I buy an ad, I get leads, and it works, why not keep doing it? And why do I need this content you are talking about?"

Viator held up a hand. "Let me correct you on your idea of digital ads.

Yes, you buy an ad, but that doesn't guarantee a lead. It only means that you have a chance for the ad to show when someone searches for something related to or close to the topic of your ad. They still have to click on it and 'convert' before you can say 'they are working.' But don't worry, I will explain the content part in due time."

About that moment, Viator waved to someone who had walked in the shop. He excused himself from the table and walked away. A few moments later, he came back with a companion. "I want to introduce you to Bob Hoffman. Bob was in the advertising business for years and was the CEO of two independent ad agencies. He is also a prolific author and commentator on the subject of advertising and digital advertising. I'm glad I saw him, as he can explain what we saw outside better than anyone I know."

Bob shook my hand and slid into the booth next to Viator. "You see, online advertising is different from traditional advertising in one fundamental way. In traditional advertising, you, as the advertiser, buy space from a publisher—like your local newspaper—because your prospective clients, like Joe Smith, are likely to read it. You buy a page in next week's edition, and you can see your ad right there in the newspaper.

"Online advertising is largely bought differently. In simple terms, there's technology that knows you're looking for someone like Joe Smith. When someone like Joe Smith shows up at a website, that website sends a message to the world saying, 'I have someone like Joe Smith here. Who wants him?' and an auction is held. If your technology comes up with the best bid, your ad is served to someone like Joe Smith. This all takes place in about a quarter of a second." He snapped his fingers for emphasis. "You often don't control where on the web your ad may appear. Your ad can appear anywhere your technology thinks it finds a person with the characteristics of Joe Smith."[1]

He continued. "You know, 'display ads [or banner ads] are usually reported to have an overall click rate of about five clicks in ten thousand ads served.' And if that isn't bad enough, three out of five of those clicks are likely to be mistakes."[2]

Viator chimed in too. "Think about trying to read a publications article on your phone, and the ad comes right at the most critical part. You see the little close button, but when you 'click' it, it opens a new tab, and you realize you didn't click the close icon, but 'fat fingered' the ad instead."

I thought for a moment about how frustrating that was and how many times that had happened to me. To think of the money wasted by a fellow small business on those accidental clicks almost made me sick to my stomach.

Viator leaned forward. "If you think that was bad, let me tell you about ad fraud and how rampant it is. Cyber criminals engage in ad fraud when they use digital channels to defraud businesses no matter the size. People like you think they are buying ads when they are buying nothing!"

Bob nodded. "The reason ad fraud has become pervasive is twofold. First, to a large degree, advertisers no longer buy advertising directly from the people who display the advertising. And second, the system by which they buy advertising is largely incomprehensible.[3]

"Complexity is a fraudster's friend. When a system is complex, bad actors have more opportunities to insert themselves into the process, and therefore, more opportunities to act fraudulently. Complex systems also make it much more difficult for buyers to know where their money is going, or at what point it is disappearing."[4]

"Well, it sounds like running a display ad on a website would be worthless then," I said, folding my arms across my chest.

"Well, yes and no." Viator held out his hands. "You see, much like anything, it depends on the circumstances and the site. If there is a niche publication your prospects read and visit all the time, it might be worth it. But on the other hand, to run an ad just to be running one and not knowing where it's showing up at, then yes, that's just stupid."

I thought for a moment and sipped my drink. "What about advertising on Google?"

"Well, it depends on which side of the house you are talking about.

Bob alluded to the Google Display Network, which is a dumpster fire fueled by fraud," Viator explained.

"If you are talking about the Google Search Network (GSN), or the text ads usually seen at the top, bottom, or both of the search results page (SERPs), above the organic listings. These ads look similar to organic search listings except for the tag 'Sponsored,' which, according to Google, is to help ensure that the user can distinguish ads from organic listings. Fortunately—or unfortunately—only half the searchers can tell the difference between a paid ad and an organic listing."

Bob tapped the table twice. "Google makes its money by misdirection. They're geniuses at it. When you type a phrase in their search box, the first results you get are all ads, not search results. Their search engine business is founded on the idea of misdirection; create a paid search result that seems to a consumer to be close enough to a natural search result to be believable. This is the essence of their business."[5]

Viator hummed in agreement. "PPC ads have been used a lot by businesses of all sizes to attract their searchers and prospects to their websites. However, just as we saw next door, depending too much on PPC can be risky in the long run. Because PPC ads are based on an auction system, the price can increase for no apparent reason. My advice is to use it sparingly."

I was beginning to understand more, but I still had questions for Bob and Viator. "What about social media advertising?"

Both Bob and Viator just shook their heads.

Bob spoke up first. "No one should trust Meta (formerly Facebook); they flat-out lie."

"Yes, it reminds me of the quote often attributed to Mark Twain, 'There are three kinds of lies: lies, [expletive] lies, and statistics.'" Viator exhaled slowly. "Meta falls right in the middle."

"You are 100% correct," Bob said. "Here is the proof: in 2017, Facebook claimed it reached 41 million Americans between the ages of 18 and 24. Even if they *had* reached every American between 18 and 24, they'd still be 10 million short. There were only 31 million of them in existence.[6]

"When questioned, Facebook offered this explanation, 'They [the metrics] are designed to estimate how many people in a given area are eligible to see an ad a business might run. They are not designed to match population or census estimates.' Honestly, I'd call that further proof they are blatant liars!"

Viator said, "Some people will tell you they are great, and I'm not saying that social media marketing doesn't work for people, but frankly, I haven't seen enough proof that it *does* work to plant my flag in their camp.

"You can upload your client's phone numbers or email list to Facebook, and it will probably recognize about half of them. Then it can take that list and build a Lookalike Audience to target. However, the problem is that you need a list of 500 to 5,000 people to upload into the system. If you are a coffee shop like this—" Viator motioned to their surroundings. "—you may have that many names. However, if you are a small business that serves fewer people but at a higher cost, having 250 names might be a stretch."

Bob cleared his throat. "I'm going to have to go soon, but I want to leave you with some food for thought. You see, Google and Facebook are known as 'walled gardens.' Walled gardens are online environments in which the publishers try to control our access to websites and apps. It's a way to keep us in their corral. Despite the ongoing and seemingly never-ending trail of scandals that these two companies have engendered, advertisers see these walled gardens as safe havens from the corruption and confusion of the programmatic online ad world. To some degree, there is logic to this.[7]

"But Google and Facebook contain another form of peril. They refuse to adhere to the same standards of third-party verification that other media adhere to. When you advertise on their sites, you have to accept their word for how many people you are reaching and how long you are reaching them. To say that their metrics are not reliable is an understatement of magnificent proportions. Procter & Gamble, the world's largest advertiser, recently established its own database of 1.5 billion people because it says it cannot trust the data it gets from Facebook and Google. Facebook recently settled a lawsuit for tens of millions of dollars in which advertisers accused it of over-representing time spent on its video content by as much as 900%."[8]

And with that, Bob slid out of the booth and shrugged. I thanked him for opening my eyes and helping me understand it all. We shook hands once more, then he walked away.

Viator leaned forward in his seat again, meeting my eyes with an earnest gaze. "I want you to realize these large tech companies are not a friend to small businesses—at least, not like they once were."

He whipped out his phone and brought up an article on POLITICO. The article read:

> A lobbying group funded by Amazon and Google claims to represent thousands of U.S. small businesses as it opposes legislation that would clamp down on the tech industry's giants.
>
> But dozens of those small businesses say they've never heard of the Connected Commerce Council.
>
> The four-year-old group listed about 5,000 small businesses in its membership directory before it removed that document from its website late last month. When POLITICO contacted 70 of those businesses, 61 said they were not members of the group and many added that they were not familiar with the organization.[9]

My jaw dropped as I read the article. I was utterly shocked. Shakily, I returned Viator's phone to him.

Viator told me that CNBC also looked into the lobbying group and found several businesses that were supposed to be affiliated with them and weren't. "The bottom line is, it's about making them money at your expense. I want you to think about this for a moment: if you are not paying for it, you're not the customer. You're the product being sold."

I thought for a moment, and everything became so clear. "What you're saying is that all these 'free services' are really capitalizing on me, my family, friends, neighbors, and everyone around the world?"

"Ding ding ding, we have a winner, folks!" Viator said, tapping a spoon against his cup. "And this isn't limited to just social media. Anyone running powerful ad tech and tracking information is also doing it."

I leaned into the table. "So what you are saying is, there are businesses like mine running this technology?"

"Yes." His tone took on a sincere note. "Now, it's not all bad; it's just that with great power also comes great responsibility."

I sat back, thinking about it all. The sheer enormity of the odds stacked against me almost made me want to give up.

I picked up my cup to savor the last bit, and in the reflection of its remnants, I could see the reflection of Otto and Constanze. I lowered my cup and looked around, and I didn't see them. I figured my mind was playing tricks on me as this place was strange enough.

Viator must have picked up on the expression that crossed my face as he looked at me and said urgently, "What did you see?"

I looked back into my cup, puzzled, and murmured, "I thought I saw Otto and Constanze, but they aren't here."

Viator picked up his cup, tossed back the last bit, and stood. "We need to keep moving. I bet they split up to cover more ground, and those two must be in the area. I just hope they don't know exactly where we are. They can't catch up to us, or we are sunk!"

4 | The Plan

As we left the 9-to-5 Grind, we walked back up the street to the digital marketing district. This area was filled with walk-up windows where people were placing their orders. Viator and I joined the line under the blue, red, yellow, and green sign.

"We are in this line because sometimes we need a little boost to help get you going," Viator explained. "However, there is a difference between using the boost to our advantage and thinking the boost is all you need to the point that it consumes you. Look around you. You see the suits, the small businesses, and the folks that look drained. The suits are using the enterprise money; as Bob alluded, they have enough to burn. The small business people like you are using digital marketing to get a boost. However, some of these have become reliant on digital marketing and have nothing else to show for it, so they keep putting money into it hoping it will get them leads and sales. Therefore, it becomes a race to the bottom while the giants keep taking their dollars."

I stood there and watched the same scene as before. Then I remembered that Viator hadn't explained exactly what we were looking at. So I asked him to describe it.

"Those small boxes are clicks on their ads. The ones that vanished immediately were people who clicked on the ad and then quickly clicked off. The ones who stay a bit longer are the ones that might be getting what they are looking for. The ones changing and transforming are the actual leads or real sales."

When it was our turn, we approached the counter and set up an ad account. Then Viator led me away from the counter. "Why not start running an ad now?" I asked.

Viator said, "We could have, but it would have been a total waste of time, effort, and money. You see, if we ran an ad now, we would just be driving the traffic to the front page of your website. While this may work for a few, the front page can rarely be specific enough to drive any meaningful conversions. Your mind is headed in the right direction; we just aren't there yet. There are still many more things we need in place before we can pull the trigger on an ad."

"Okay," I said with frustration and hesitation in my voice. I began to wonder if I had chosen the right path or if I should just cut my losses and walk away. But at the same time, I still had no way of knowing how to get out of here and back home.

We walked in silence until we came to a pair of buildings; the sign on one said Initrode and the other said Initech. Viator stopped on the sidewalk and gestured at the buildings behind him. "If I gave you the opportunity to buy this, would you? Or would you rather rent it?"

I looked between the buildings, trying to discern their quality. "What is the cost difference between the two long-term?"

"Negligible."

"I guess I would rather own it if I could afford it."

"That is the correct answer! You see, just like buying this building, having something that is yours and you can fully control is the key to everything. As Joe Pulizzi says, 'Don't build your business on rented land!' No matter what you do, when it comes to marketing online, anytime you can own something, the better off you are."

He went on to say, "I have spoken with numerous people and businesses over the years who think that their social media page is their website. I'm here to tell you that it is *not* your website! That is a page on someone else's website! Therefore, you have to invest and build your own so you have somewhere to drive people to. Everything should come back to your website with a message you can control."

I chuckled. "Get on a soap box much?"

He just laughed. "Sometimes, when I'm passionate about something. And I happen to be very passionate about that subject."

We walked a little further. Viator approached the door of the building and opened the door. A sign on the door read, "The Office Space: Place to Stop, Collaborate, and Get Working." He looked back and said, "Are you coming?"

As I walked in, it was a beautiful space, with rows of desks with people working, small offices on the left wall, a kitchen area with a bar and barstools that stretched across, and a larger room on their right.

Viator breathed a sigh of relief as he led us into the larger room. "We should be safe here for now, at least."

I squinted at him and crossed my arms, watching as Viator sank into a chair at the long conference table dominating the center of the room. "I need some details on what is going on. Who are Otto, Constanze, and Phoebus? Why are they after me or you, and how is all this that you are showing me going to help my business!"

Viator shifted in his chair, frowning. "Otto and Constanze are here to keep you from achieving your goals, and they want you to stay right where you are, no matter how miserable you are. Phoebus has a similar goal, but he wants to keep you in fear of making a change and paralyzed with doubt. The bottom line is, all three are after you simply because I'm helping you. Like I said when I met you on the bench, you need to trust me, as this isn't my first rodeo."

"Ok, that explains who they are, and I guess why they are after me, but you have yet to tell me how you are going to help my business grow," I said, obviously frustrated.

Viator stood and went to a whiteboard and started scribbling on it. When he had finished, he said, "Look here, this is everything we are going to do."

The board read:

1. Develop a Marketing Strategy and Plan
   - Target Market and Buyer Persona
   - Content Types and Counts
2. Build and Optimize the Website
3. Blog
4. Service and Geo-landing Pages
5. Social Proof
6. SEO
7. Social Media
8. Email Marketing
9. Video

1. Develop a Marketing Strategy and Plan
    - Target Market and Buyer Persona
    - Content Types and Counts
2. Build and Optimize the Website
3. Blog
4. Service Pages/Landing Pages/Geo-landing pages
5. Social Proof, Testimonials, and Reviews
6. SEO
7. Social Media
8. Email Marketing
9. Video

As he pointed to each item on the board, he said, "We are going to start with a solid plan. We'll to look at your ideal buyers, what your website needs to look like, how much content should be produced, and what types of content will compel your buyers to convert."

I dropped my arms to my sides and leaned against the edge of the conference table. "Ok, I get some of this, but can you elaborate on each, so I have a better idea of what I need to be doing?"

"Of course. What do you want to know first?"

TARGET MARKET AND BUYER PERSONAS

I hummed, thinking. "Well, I guess I want to better understand what the target market and buyer personas are, since they are first on the list."

"That is an excellent question and a great place to start. Many people don't understand what it is or the importance of them.

TARGET MARKET

"You see, your target market is a bit broader than the buyer persona. It takes into account the people who are most likely to employ you for your services. If you are a business-to-business (B2B) enterprise, it's going to focus on the industry, niches, or vertices. If you are more business-to-consumer-oriented (B2C), it will focus more on geographical service areas, for example. And if you are in a rural area like us, it will focus heavily on the geographical location."

Uncapping his marker again, he wrote the following list on the board:

> - Analyze your service(s)
> - What is your competition doing that is the same or different than you are
> - The geographical features of your ideal clientele or your service area

- Analyze your service(s)
- What is your competition doing that is similar to or different from your approach?
- The geographical features of your ideal clientele or your service area

BUYER PERSONA

Viator capped the marker again and turned back to me. "Essentially, a buyer persona is a fancy way of identifying your ideal client. A buyer persona will often include the following:

- Age
- Geographic location
- Gender
- Income
- Occupation
- Job Title
- Industry
- Hobbies
- Interests

Pain points and key problems they are coming to you to solve (also known as psychographics)

"Now, based on the answers to this list, we can use target markets and buyer personas to help us make all decisions moving forward. For example, I love the color red, but if my prospects see the color red as a negative, then maybe I shouldn't use it. Does that make sense?"

"Yeah," I replied, nodding. "It does. What you're saying is that I don't always need to go with what I like; it's more about what will resonate best with my clientele."

"Exactly!" he exclaimed. "So many businesses go with what they like or what they want, ignoring what the client wants or is looking for. They think, 'Because I like it, my clients will like it too.' Unfortunately, that isn't always the case."

Viator tapped the table with the cap of his marker. "Now, let's dive a little deeper into the buyer persona and think about a negative one."

NEGATIVE BUYER PERSONA

"A negative persona?"

"Yes," he said. "A negative persona can be as helpful as a positive one—sometimes even more so. You see, many people want to say that their ideal person is anyone who can pay for their services. While that's great, it's not ideal. Just because a person has the money to pay for your services doesn't mean they are a good fit to work with. So, tell me about some of the clients you have worked with in the past that you would *never* want to work with again."

I thought for a moment and started reciting story after story of people who were difficult to deal with and who made the whole experience not worth the money.

Viator listened for a while, nodding, then stopped me with a raised hand. "See, these are the people we need to make sure we communicate are *not* a good fit. Sometimes it's coming out and saying it point blank. Other times we have to dance around it, and sometimes you just have to tell them to their faces that they aren't going to be a good fit."

CONTENT TYPES AND COUNTS

"Ok, well—" I motioned back to the whiteboard. "What do you mean content types and counts? Are you going to teach people about math on my website?"

"No," he replied with a chuckle. "The content types and counts refer to the type of content that will work best and how many pieces of each that need to be produced."

He steepled his fingers for a moment, thinking. "Think about it like this: the plan is like a blueprint for a house, and the content type and count are more like a material list and material count. They give you an idea of whether you'll need bricks or wood for your house, and how much of each thing you'll need. Now, this can change as we get into it, but it gives us a baseline to start with."

BUILD AND OPTIMIZE WEBSITE

I nodded slowly, picturing the house-building metaphor. "I think I understand—but explain the website part to me. I mean, I already have a website," I said proudly.

"Really?"

"Yep, I got my father's brother's nephew's cousin's former roommate to build it."

Viator seemed to wince. "Ah, well, that is great, and that is likely a good start, but what I have found is that when you get someone like that to build it, they don't take into account everything your *particular* website needs."

Smiling apologetically, he motioned for me to sit next to him at the table. "Let's take a look at your current site and run some tests on it." Viator waved his hands in the air above the conference table and opened a screen that floated in the air in front of us. Then he went through my site and explained everything as he evaluated it by a specific checklist:

- How fast does it load?
- Is it a responsive design or mobile-friendly?
- What was it built on or in?
- Does it meet basic accessibility requirements for font sizes, color contrast, skip navigation, etc.?
- How does it currently rank on an SEO audit?
- Are there technical issues with the site?
- Does it have a sitemap?
- Do the pages have meta descriptions?
- Does it have a blog or a place to blog?
- Are there dedicated landing pages?
- Is the text on the pages more about the business or how the business can help the searcher?

As you might expect, the site came back with several issues that I had no clue existed. With disgust and a tinge of anger in my voice, I said,

"Well, that is somewhat disheartening. I would have thought that it would have fared better in your tests than that."

Viator shook his head. "Don't be discouraged. You would be surprised at how often I see this. From DIYers to cheap hires, 'free' and 'cheap' online builders, and 'professionals,' they all can have issues. Even sites I have helped with in the past don't pass the sniff test now. I want to make something clear as well. This isn't to say that all the other sites and options are bad. I just see it more often than I would like to admit."

CONTENT DEVELOPMENT

"When it comes to developing the content (that is, the text, images, graphics, infographics, audio, and video) for a site, there are a few basic items you need to have and think about:

- Keep all your text focused on the searcher and write it as if you were speaking to one person directly—because you are.
- When you or anyone else writes a blog, you want to think about whether this answers the searcher's question. This is sometimes referred to as the "They Ask, You Answer" framework developed by Marcus Sheridan.
- When you develop your landing pages and geo-landing pages, again, you will want to follow a framework. For these, I like to use a modified version of the "Story Brand" framework developed by Donald Miller.
- You will also need to have social proof in the form of testimonials, reviews, and possibly case studies."

SEO

"What about SEO?"

Viator hummed. "That is a great question. Do you actually know what it is and what it means?"

I shrugged my shoulders. "I think I do."

"Ok, let's hit the highlights, and then I can go into more detail later. There is a good definition I like to use by Search Engine Land.

SEO stands for "search engine optimization." In simple terms, it means the process of improving your site to increase its visibility when people search for products or services related to your business in Google, Bing, [Yahoo!], and other search engines. The better visibility your pages have in search results, the more likely you are to garner attention and attract prospective and existing customers to your business.

"Now, for our purposes, I want to expand on it. SEO can be broken down into three parts, On-page, Off-page, and Technical SEO."

Viator placed a blue marker on the table between us. "On-page SEO covers everything you do on your website to improve its competitiveness on the search engine results pages (SERPs). These are the factors that you have complete control over because you own the website."

He placed a red marker on the table next to the blue one. "Off-page SEO is about creating backlinks and boosting your SERP ranking externally. In other words, it's about link-building. By definition, link-building is the actions you take to help increase the amount of inbound traffic or links from other sites to your website. The more connections to your website, the more Google will recognize your content and enhance your rankings.

"Now, the SEO community is somewhat divided on how well backlinks work these days and how valuable Google and the other search engines are. But I believe if they demonstrate the value of your content, show the trustworthiness of your content, and help the web crawlers in finding their way to your website, then it's worth the effort of building backlinks."

A final, green marker took its place beside the other two. "Technical SEO covers everything related to the structure of your website. It helps you meet the requirements that allow search engines to crawl your site and find their way through your content and pages." Viator smiled. "Is this all making sense?"

"Yes," I said. "But I still have questions."

"Questions are good—so jot them down, and I can address them in more detail later."

SOCIAL MEDIA

Viator spun his chair to face me and crossed one leg over the other. "Let's quickly talk about social media. It is great if you use it to your advantage. Here are a couple of things to think about:

- Be sure to keep the 'social' in social media. It's not all about your services. It's about showing the human side of the business and being there to answer questions.
- Build influence. In other words, be sociable and helpful.
- Social media is rented land.
- Use it to help promote helpful content on your website and drive followers to your website."

EMAIL NEWSLETTERS

"I think I understand what you're talking about when it comes to social media, but what about email newsletters and email marketing? I bet I get more than 100 emails every day, and some I don't even open." I frowned. "I just don't know if those work anymore."

"Think about this: if you received an email that had actual value and wasn't all promotional and 'buy buy buy,' would you be more inclined to open and read it?" Viator asked.

"Yeah, I guess."

"Ok, then create the email newsletter that you would want to read. You see, they are easily one of the best ways to help cultivate relationships with potential clients and keep current clients updated with helpful content." Viator looked at me and smiled. "You look tired. Are you ready to call it a day?"

"Sure," I said. "This has definitely been a lot to think about. I guess it's just harder for me to see how all this is going to work."

"All in due time," he said, clapping a hand on my shoulder. "All in due time."

With that Viator pulled out his phone and the next thing I knew he said I booked you a hotel room. I will ride with you to the hotel and make sure you get in ok.

Viator helped me get checked in, and I headed to my hotel room he had gotten for me. I walked in and plopped down on the bed, exhausted but with my mind racing.

I laid there a while before rising to get ready for bed. Passing the mirror, I saw Otto, Constanze, and Phoebus looking back at me. I spun around and, finding the room empty, I looked back to the mirror. The three people were still there. I figured this must be some sort of crazy dream—but then Constanze spoke.

"You know what you have is good enough, right?" she said.

Otto nodded. "Yes, it is. You spent all that money getting that website built; it would be a shame to waste it."

Then Phoebus chimed in. "You know how hard it was to do it the first time. All that time and work. Do you really want to go through that again?"

Before I could reply, I blinked and all I could see was my own reflection staring back at me.

As I lay back down, I couldn't help but think about what they had said. My mind was slowly filling with doubt—doubt that I would get back home, doubt that I could turn the business around, doubt that Viator could actually help me. And with that, I drifted into a fitful sleep.

5 | Your Website is Your Foundation

It is not the beauty of a building you should look at; it's the construction of the foundation that will stand the test of time.

— David Allan Coe

Nothing is more powerful than an idea whose time has come.

— Victor Hugo

The following day, I woke up and made my way back to The 9-to-5 Grind coffee shop where I was to meet Viator. The sun gently filtered through the coffee shop's windows as I stepped inside. As I scanned the room, my eyes landed on Viator, comfortably settled in the same booth as yesterday. He looked at home, like it was a second office to him.

I sat down, and a cup was already sitting there for me. I took a sip as Viator spoke.

"How did you sleep?" he inquired, his voice carrying a genuine concern.

I shrugged, trying to mask any lingering fatigue. "Okay, I guess," I replied, a hint of weariness unintentionally seeping into my words.

Viator's perceptive gaze didn't waver as he studied me intently. "You look tired still," he remarked.

For a brief moment, I debated whether to admit my weariness, but then I dismissed it. "No, I'm good," I assured him.

Viator peered at me as if he was looking through me. "You are having doubts, aren't you?"

"Well, now that you mention it, I did have a crazy dream." I then proceeded to tell him the events that happened last night.

With a look of despair and panic, he said, "That was no dream. That is one of their favorite tactics. They like to catch you off guard and plant the seeds."

As I spoke, my voice trembled with uncertainty. "Well, I guess I do have some doubts about it, if I'm honest," Pausing for a moment, I took a deep breath, gathering my thoughts. "I mean, what you said yesterday makes sense, but at the same time I did spend a lot of time and money in the past, and obviously, things aren't working. How do I know that it will work this time?"

"I see your point, and questioning things isn't necessarily bad, but do you remember what I told you when you asked me to help you grow your business?"

"Yes," I replied, "There were three steps: Ask for help, know that what I have done might not be the best solution, and be open-minded."

"That is right. Now, your self-doubt is preventing you from looking at other solutions and being open-minded. So the question becomes: What do you want to do? What is your ultimate goal? What is your exit plan when you decide to retire or move on? In other words, do you want to grow your business or let it get stagnant and wither away?"

"Way to get right to the point there."

Viator leaned back in his chair, a knowing smile playing on his lips. "Well, I have to," he began, with a voice filled with years of experience. "You see, I have worked with hundreds of businesses over the years, and without fail, they all start out wanting what I refer to as a 'brochure site.' These are the simple sites that answer the five W's: or the 'who, what, when, where, and why/how' of the business. These same businesses will obsess about the front page, making it perfect. They also worry about things that don't matter in the grand scheme of things.

"I'm not saying that the appearance and navigation of the site aren't important, because they are—just as the colors, logo, fonts, and design are. But what truly matters is the material itself, how it's arranged, and how it motivates purchasers to take action."

"Think about it like this, you go to a restaurant and look at the menu, pick out what you want to eat, and the wait staff brings it to your table. You will eat with your eyes first. If the plate looks good, then it will likely taste good. However, just because it looks good doesn't mean it will taste good and curb your hunger. Your website is the same way.I

It can look good, but if it doesn't answer the searcher's questions, it won't matter."

I was beginning to understand a little bit more.

Viator leaned forward, "When it comes to a website, most people will first go to a search engine." With a chuckle, he added, "I have even seen people search for their own website instead of typing it in—but I digress. The point is," he emphasized, their tone growing serious, "when a user conducts a search on a search engine, like Google, they are presented with a list of links. And each link serves as a gateway to the web page that best aligns with their search criteria. In their book *Inbound Marketing*, Brian Halligan and Dharmesh Shah explained that a searcher could be taken to 'a page with information about your product, a blog article, or any other web page on your site.'

"Yet another way to think about it is like reading the *Holy Bible*. One typically doesn't start with Genesis and read through to Revelation. You jump in and around. Your website is the same way. Most people will not start on the front page and go through every page. They might start on a landing page, go to a blog post, then to the front, and finish up on a contact page. The bottom line is, the journey will be different for everyone; therefore, we have to make sure that we make the site the best it can be."

Viator inquired, his voice tinged with a mix of seriousness and concern, "Do you see now why I got to the point of making sure you wanted help?"

His words echoed in the air, lingering with a weight that called for introspection. As I thought about his question, his unwavering determination to ensure my commitment became increasingly apparent.

Viator continued, his voice steady, "I will level with you. We still have a lot of work to do, and if you're not on board, then it's a waste of time for both of us." He stood, lifting his cup. "I'm going to get a refill. You should think about what you really want while I'm gone."

I sat there and tried to think about everything Viator had told me and asked me. By the time he came back a few minutes later, I had made my decision.

As he sat, Viator asked, "What are you thinking? Are you ready to move forward or throw in the towel?"

"Let's give this a shot. I should be able to see some traction quickly, right?"

Viator leaned forward, a thoughtful expression crossing his face. "Well, yes and no. What we do isn't easy, and it is very much a long-term play. There are some things along the way that we can do to make things move a little faster, but in my experience, it takes about 6 to 12 months for things to really start happening."

I felt the wash of doubt come back over me again; 6 to 12 months was way too long.

Viator leaned forward, there seemed to almost be a twinkle in his eyes, "This process is like having a baby. It usually takes a good three months before you really see any signs of things going on. Then by the six-month mark, you really start noticing things. Typically by nine months, you've delivered a nice little bundle of leads and sales that came organically through the website."

I smiled as he relayed the story, and it made sense. After that, I felt much more comfortable about the process and told him as much.

Back in The Office Space, we sat in front of the whiteboard.

"It's like this: if you are going to grow your business, then you have to think about your marketing. And it doesn't matter if it's with traditional media or digital. Everything has to come back to the website." Viator uncapped his marker. "Follow me?"

"Yes," I remarked.

"Ok, so your website needs to tick off six things to be effective," he said while writing them on the board:

1. Design and Development
2. Copy
3. Basic Accessibility Requirements
4. Is it easy to navigate and do things "flow"
5. Is it responsive or mobile-friendly
6. Is it designed to convert

When he had finished, he turned to me again. "Does your site meet all those requirements? If you say no, then you need an update and refresh."

I protested, saying, "But I just did this…"

He interrupted me and cut his hand through the air. "It doesn't matter! It doesn't matter if you finished it last week or last year. The point is, whomever you got to do your site either didn't know what they were doing, didn't want to bring up these questions, or frankly just didn't care. Regardless, these requirements must be met."

DESIGN AND DEVELOPMENT

"Now, before I go any further, I want to make one thing perfectly clear: there is a difference between a designer and a developer."

"A designer is a graphic artist who has the expertise to make the site look good, will help to maintain your brand, and craft visual impact. A developer is going to be more behind the scenes, making it all work. They will understand the languages of the web and how to make sure your site works as intended. And if you find one person that can do both well—not just say they can—that is rare indeed."

Viator went to a bookshelf standing on the wall opposite the whiteboard and pulled a book. As he brought it back to our side of the table, I could see post-it notes stuck throughout. He opened it and handed it to me to read. "Most websites fail and fail miserably."

MOST WEBSITES FAIL

The book was *Making Websites Win* by Ben Jesson and Karl Blanks, and the passage he pointed out said,

> Most websites lose. Almost all of them.
>
> Many of them never make a profit. Like chocolate teapots, they look nice but flop as soon as you pour hot customers into them.

"In other words, many sites are designed with what the business wants on there and not what the client wants. While yes, it is your website, the question becomes whether you want your website to cater to you or to get searchers to become your clients?"

I sat across from Viator, my mind filled with aspirations of attracting more clients to my business. With a hint of uncertainty, I voiced my concern, seeking his guidance. "Obviously, I want more clients. But what you are saying is that my website doesn't need to be about me?"

"No," he replied, "it can still be about you, your business, and represent your brand. However, we must ensure that we help the searchers find what they are looking for and show them how you are there to help them. You and your site have to be the guide and not the hero. Your prospects and clients are the heroes."

LAYOUT AND TYPOGRAPHY

"When you have someone help design your website, you want to think about how people interact with a website and also how they traditionally prefer things.

"For this, I want to refer back to the late David Ogilvy, who was the founder of Ogilvy & Mather and known as the 'Father of Advertising.' In his book *Ogilvy on Advertising*, he wrote:

> Readers look first at the illustration, then at the headline, then at the copy. So put these elements in that order—illustration at the top, headline under the illustration, copy under the headline. This follows the normal order of scanning, which is from top to bottom. If you put the headline *above* the illustration, you are

asking people to scan in an order which does not fit their habit.

On the average, headlines *below* the illustration are read by 10 percent more people than headlines *above* the illustration.

"Ogilvy also said, 'Good typography *helps* people read your copy, while bad typography prevents them from doing so.' He is also quoted as saying, 'You may think that I exaggerate the importance of good typography. You may ask if I have ever heard a housewife say that she bought a new detergent because the advertisement was set in Caslon. No. But do you think an advertisement can sell if nobody can read it? You can't save souls in an empty church.'

Here are some additional points on typography and body text design:

- Don't use all capitals for headlines, as they are harder to read as the brain has to read them letter by letter.
- Don't superimpose headlines on your photos or images. As any good designer will tell you, this is one of the hardest things to pull off effectively.
- Don't put a period at the end of headlines; it represents a complete stop, and the reader may never read your copy.
- A two-line subhead between your headline and body text piques the reader's interest.
- Headings and subheadings indicate the beginning of sections and subsections.
- Consider limiting your opening paragraph to around 11 words.
- Put key points in **bold** or *italics* to call attention to them.
- Use numbered lists and bullets to help the searcher when they skim your text.

COPY

Viator pointed to the whiteboard at the word "Copy."

"Your copy will include your text, photos, images, graphics, infographics, audio files, and videos. Now, a graphic designer can help you with some of this, but you may want to consider getting someone who is an excellent writer, such as a journalist, English major, et cetera to help with the text. You see, a good writer can take a few bullet points or a few things you throw at them and spin it into an article or copy on the page that will make a searcher beat down your door to hire you."

CONTENT IS KING

Viator gripped the marker tightly, then swiftly scribbled, "Content Is King." He then pulled out his phone and did a quick search for the exact phrase. He handed it to me and said, "a look at this," he urged, his voice brimming with enthusiasm. "Notice how many results there are."

I saw the all-too-familiar interface of the search engine. I scanned the page and was astounded to see about four billion results!

"Now, look at who is most often credited with coining it and when."

Most of the results cited Bill Gates, and the year recorded was January 1996.

"Now check out what the article says."

I clicked through and began to skim it:

> Content is where I expect much of the real money will be made on the Internet, just as it was in broadcasting.

> The television revolution that began half a century ago [the 1950s] spawned a number of industries, including the manufacturing of TV sets, but the long-term winners were those who used the medium to deliver information and entertainment.

> When it comes to an interactive network such as the Internet,

the definition of "content" becomes very wide…

One of the exciting things about the Internet is that anyone with a PC and a modem can publish whatever content they can create. In a sense, the Internet is the multimedia equivalent of the photocopier. It allows material to be duplicated at low cost, no matter the size of the audience.

…If people are to be expected to put up with turning on a computer to read a screen, they must be rewarded with deep and extremely up-to-date information that they can explore at will. They need to have audio, and possibly video. They need an opportunity for personal involvement that goes far beyond that offered through the letters-to-the-editor pages of print magazines.

As I finished, I handed the phone back to Viator. He asked, "Do you understand what I mean when I say 'Content is King?'"

I nodded, "Yes, it's somewhat unsettling how accurate Bill Gates' predictions have proven to be," I remarked, a tinge of awe in my voice. The foresight and vision displayed by someone like Bill Gates highlight the rapid advancements and transformative nature of technology, leaving us in awe of what the future holds."

"I agree. I have often wondered where he got a flux capacitor and kept his Delorian," Viator joked. He continued "I often tell prospects and clients that I meet with that having a good-looking site is only one part of the puzzle. If you want to be found on the Internet, you must have content that the search engines can find and index—and it can't be crappy content for the sake of having content.

"All the search engines update their algorithms to help provide better results for the searchers. With those updates, there are things that they will throw out, such as:

- Duplicate, thin, or low-quality content
- Content that lacks authority or trustworthiness
- Low-quality, user-generated content
- Content farming
- "What they prefer is:
- Long-form content that presents topics and ideas in-depth
- Content that provides the best solution
  to searchers' questions

"Does that make sense?" he asked.

"Yeah, I think so. It sure does sound like a lot of work, though."

"Well, as I said at the start, it's not an easy journey. But once you get to the end, you will be rewarded handsomely."

HOW TO WRITE FOR SEARCHERS

"That is a good starting point and stopping point for the content itself. Now let's talk about how the text needs to sound to help searchers, prospects, and clients out."

Viator flipped to another page in the *Making Websites Win* book and pointed to this highlighted statement: "Teachers and bosses may like intelligent-sounding text, but readers prefer text that's easy to understand."

He said, "Using your target audience and buyer personas, we can determine who you need to write to. You can't use industry jargon if you are writing to a layperson. However, if you are writing to an industry professional, jargon might be perfectly acceptable. The bottom line is to know your audience and write to their level.

"When you are writing the text or having it written, just like the layout and typography, there are some things that you will want to do:

- Your headlines need to engage searchers quickly.
- The content should be written with the searcher in mind, utilizing "you" language rather than "we."
- Follow the KISS (Keep It Simple, Stupid) principle: keep it simple, easy to understand, and free of jargon.
- Sentences and paragraphs should be brief and to the point, with one thought per sentence and one idea per paragraph.
- There should always be a call to action, or people will not act.

Viator leaned forward, his voice carrying a sense of conviction. "Something else you need to consider is that your website is never truly done."

"Never done?" I echoed, seeking clarification.

Viator nodded, a knowing smile playing on his lips. "If you ask a 'car guy' if their car is ever finished, most will say no. There is always something you can fine-tune, modify, change, or swap out. Your website is no different."

BASIC ACCESSIBILITY REQUIREMENTS

Gesturing back toward the whiteboard, he said, "Let's dive into basic accessibility requirements. In other words, did the designer and developer take into account the accommodations legally required by the ADA (the Americans with Disabilities Act) Standards for Accessible Design? Did they think about the font sizes, color contrast, skip navigation, etc.?"

"The late Cindy Li famously said, 'We're all just temporarily abled.' Profound statement, is it not?"

"Yeah, I guess."

"Hmm, it sounds like you aren't convinced. Let me give you a few examples:

- As we all get older, our eyesight tends to fail, and we need glasses or 'readers' to help. If your target audience is this demographic, you might want to consider having a larger font to eliminate friction for the user.
- Color blindness is a condition typically found in men, who can't see the difference between certain colors, such as red and green, but it can also happen with blue and yellow. Therefore, if your site uses red and green text or text without significant contrast, it will be harder for someone to read, adding friction to the process.
- Another would be if you injure or break your hand or arm and cannot use the keyboard and mouse with your dominant hand. If your site isn't configured properly to allow for 'tabbing through,' then you are adding friction for the user.
- One other example isn't a disability per se, but more of a thought about how we interact with our phone and mobile websites, so picture this: You are left-hand dominant. Still, most hamburger menus (the three bars signifying a menu) are on the right side. You then have to reach your thumb across the screen or use your right hand to tap it. Again, you just added a whole heap of friction for that southpaw.

"Does that clear things up a bit for you?"

"That is certainly an eye opener for sure! I had never thought about any of that before."

"Oh, it gets better. There have been numerous lawsuits over websites not meeting accessibility standards and guidelines," he said with voice laced with a touch of concern "It's one reason why I bring it up to people—not to scare them, but to make sure they are aware of it."

With a touch of exasperation, I said, "Geez, people will sue over anything these days, won't they."

"Yep, and as the saying goes, the best defense is a good offense. With that said, here are a few things I always tell people to look at and places to find more information:

- The U.S. General Services Administration (GSA) Office has a dedicated website (Section508.gov) with a website tester and a wealth of information.
- Web Accessibility Initiative (w3.org) also has a wealth of information and a tester.

He then handed me a printout with some additional information and sources, which he seemed to pull from thin air.

NAVIGATION

"I mentioned the hamburger menu before; that's just one thing to think about when you consider site navigation. Here are a few more things you need to think about with your navigation," he said, writing these on the board.

- Five to seven top-level menu items
- Limit dropdown to a single level
- No home button or menu item
- Use layman's terms
- Leave social media off the top*

After he wrote those down, he turned to me to elaborate on each. "Now, when I help a client set up their menu structure, I do it in a Google Sheet or a spreadsheet so they can visualize the structure going across and any dropdowns below the top-level menu items. I work with them to limit the items to 5-7 options, max. If there are less than that, it looks sparse; if there are more than that, it's too many choices or it's hard to fit neatly in your menu."

Viator went to the side of the list and proceeded to write out the following list:

1. ~~Home~~
2. About (Who)
3. Services (When and what)
4. Pricing
5. Blog
6. Contact (Where and How)
7. Social Media Icons *

1. ~~Home~~
2. About (Who)
3. Services (When and What)
4. Pricing
5. Blog
6. Contact (Where and How)
7. Social Media Icons*

"That is a general list of some of the top-level items you will want to include. Now, I realize you might not be able to list pricing, but you may be able to replace it with 'Testimonials' or the like." he explained.

Viator continued, his voice filled with enthusiasm. "Additionally, I like using a spreadsheet layout that allows the client to see dropdown menus below the top-level items. And prevents the need for a tertiary dropdown or fly out. Now I realize there are edge cases, but typically you don't need them if you plan accordingly."

He then looked back at the list and struck out the bullet point that read "Home" with a firm slash of the marker. "Now, why do you think I did that?"

It definitely caught my attention, with pure curiosity I said, "I wondered why you did. It seems like it would be an important one to include."

He put his hand to his forehead and looked down. He then looked back up, sighed, and shook his head. "Lose the 'Home' menu item. You don't need it since everyone and their brother, whether they realize it or not, knows to click the logo to return to the home page. All it does is take up valuable real estate.

"Another thing clients often want to do is name the menu items by what they call each thing internally, but that only leads to confusion. Best practice is to put everything in layman's terms.

"Lastly, the social media icons. I put an asterisk here because people disagree about whether they should be at the top of your website or not. Now, I typically fall on the side that says they shouldn't be at the top. The reason being is that you did a lot of work to get someone to your website; maybe you even paid for that click. Well, if one of the first things a potential client sees are the icons for your social media accounts, they're more likely to check out your accounts—but then you've just lost them to the social media companies' websites or apps. Two hours later, they forgot what they were looking for, and they start the entire search process over again."

RESPONSIVE

"Ok, this is going to get a little bit more technical, but I want you to have a good understanding of the differences. Essentially, there are two ways a website can be presented on different devices. Those are:

- Mobile-friendly
- Responsive design

MOBILE-FRIENDLY

"We don't see these sites as much as we did in the early 2010s, but these sites were typically dedicated mobile sites that were basically shoehorned versions of the desktop version. Oftentimes these sites had to be updated independently. For better or worse, the term has become synonymous with making sure the website looks good on all devices."

RESPONSIVE DESIGN

"The second way, which is the preferred and modern way, is to develop a responsive design. In other words, the website responds independently of the size of the browser window or device it is being viewed on."

Viator paused and tossed his marker in the air, watching it flip end over end before he caught it. "Are you following the difference?"

"Yes, I think I am."

"Good! Now, the easiest way to test if your site is responsive is to open it on a desktop or laptop, then grab the side of the browser window and slide it in. The site should start folding up like someone doing origami until it looks similar to what you would see on your phone."

He slid his laptop over to me and asked me to test it on my site, my competitors', and a couple of others, which I did.

"Now, I want you to think about the people in your area. Do they have high-speed internet, broadband? Or do they have to use something else?"

"I know there are places that do and places that don't."

"Now, how many of those without direct access do you think use a cell phone to access the Internet?"

"Wow, I don't know," I responded, a hint of uncertainty in my voice. "I guess most of them."

"According to a 2021 report from the Pew Research Center, '93% of U.S. adults say they use the Internet' and '77% of U.S. adults say they have a broadband connection at home.' The same report also noted that '15% of U.S. adults say they do not use broadband at home but own smartphones.' This leads me to believe that most people without internet access at home use their mobile devices."

"Armed with that research, it helps us understand that we have to think about users trying to use your site on 'slower connections' and mobile-only devices. Therefore, you need to make sure that elements are large enough to click with a thumb without accidentally clicking something else. You should also avoid large graphics and videos that are critical to the function of the page."

DESIGNED TO CONVERT

With a determined look on his face, Viator said, "Let's talk about making sure your site is set up to convert."

"Let me tell you about something that happened to my wife and me recently," Viator said with a voice filled with amusement. "We were in a large home decor and arts-and-crafts retail store chain. This one was different from the one she would typically shop at. I needed to use the restroom, so I headed to the back wall, where the bathrooms in the stores we frequented were. But they weren't there. Knowing they had to be on one of the outside walls, I walked around the entire perimeter of the store looking for it. Finally, I got frustrated and asked someone to direct me to it. After making my way back to my wife, she asked what took me so long, and I had to explain to her that it wasn't where it was in 'our stores.' She looked at me, shook her head, and proceeded to finish her window shopping."

With a contemplative expression on Viator's face, as he posed a thought-provoking scenario. "Now, imagine if that store was a website and the goal was to go to the front page and find your services. Do you think they would have taken as much time as I did? Would they contact you for help, or would they leave and go to the next one where they are easy to find."

"That is an easy answer. They would go to the next one," I said confidently.

"Exactly, so your website needs to make it easy for people to find what they are looking for and take whatever action you want them to take," Viator replied. He went on to explain that, when it comes to designing a website, a designer will want to make it a showpiece and a work of art. This is great if you are designing a site to showcase the art, but if you want people to hire you for your services, you have to keep it simple.

He turned again and proceeded to write this on the whiteboard:

- Logo, Navigation, and Contact Information
- Slideshow
- Loss Aversion
- Value Proposition
- Guide
- Plan
- Explanatory Paragraph
- Video (optional)
- Pricing (optional)
- NASCAR Area (optional)
- Junk Drawer

Then Viator took his seat beside me and gestured to the board. "This is a modified version of the 'Building A Story Brand Wireframe.'" Propping his leg up on his knee, he sat back and began to explain.

LOGO, NAVIGATION, AND CONTACT INFORMATION

At the very top of your site, you should see your logo, navigation, and contact information. The arrangement is subjective; it just needs to be visually appealing. Some will argue that you need to have your phone number always visible. I say it depends on the industry and the target market.

SLIDESHOW

This area goes by numerous names: slideshow, image rotator, carousel, slider, or header. No matter what you call it, this is where you can put a little bit of information about what you offer.

A word of caution: You want to avoid splicing critical information across multiple slides. You see, studies have shown that clicks on slide 2+ only received 1% of clicks. They have even been shown to frustrate users.

If you choose to use a slideshow, consider placing the same text on all the slides or a looping video with no audio. Just make sure the text can be read over the images. As I mentioned before, this is one of the hardest things for a graphic designer to accomplish correctly.

LOSS AVERSION

At its core, loss aversion is a psychological bias that causes us to place more emphasis on avoiding losses than on achieving gains. Therefore, let the prospect know what you will help save them from. Illustrate the problems they have and how you can solve them.

VALUE PROPOSITION

Explain why a prospect should hire you for your services. You can bullet-point some of the benefits as well.

GUIDE

Introduce your business as the one who can help fix the prospect's problems or issues. In other words be the Obi-Wan to your prospects Luke, or be the Dumbldore to Harry Potter.

PLAN

Roll out the blueprint of how you will help the prospect and the steps they need to take to hire you.

EXPLANATORY PARAGRAPH

Explains everything in a few paragraphs.

VIDEO (OPTIONAL)

If you have a video, you can use it to explain in a different way what you said in the preceding sections.

PRICING (OPTIONAL)

This is somewhat self-explanatory, but you should always include pricing if you can, even if it's just a starting point. I will get into it more later.

NASCAR AREA (OPTIONAL)

I jokingly refer to this area as the NASCAR area. If you have ever seen one of their cars, they are covered in the logos of their sponsors. Therefore, if you have any big companies or names in your area that you have worked with, you can put those here. This helps to provide a bit of validation and social proof. You can also swap in testimonials here.

JUNK DRAWER

Just like every southern house has one, your website needs a junk drawer. This is where you will find everything from your social media profiles, billing address, links to your privacy policy and terms and conditions, etc.

CALL-TO-ACTION (CTA) BUTTONS

I stood and stretched the stiffness from my joints.

Viator smiled at me kindly. "I know I threw a lot at you today. But there are two more big pieces and two smaller pieces I want to talk about that are directly related to the website. Can you go a little longer?"

Rubbing the tightness out of my neck, I nodded. "Sure. It's a lot to take in, but let's keep going."

"Great. The first is your CTAs."

I stopped him there and asked, "Before we get too far into this, can you clarify what you mean by a CTA?"

"Of course. HubSpot defines a CTA as 'part of a webpage, advertisement, or piece of content that encourages the audience to do something. In marketing, CTAs help a business convert a visitor or reader into a lead for the sales team. CTAs can drive a variety of different actions depending on the content's goal.' In my words and for our purposes, it's basically a prompt to entice a searcher, visitor, or prospect to take some specified action. This may be to visit another page on your website, contact you, call you, sign up for your email newsletter or download something. Essentially, it's a call-to-action button. Make sense?"

"Yes, but how do you get someone to want to click on them?"

Viator started to explain the intricacies of effective website messaging, "You see, all website searchers, visitors, prospects, and clients subscribe to the WIIFM (what's in it for me) station. If the text, context, or offer on your CTA doesn't answer that, then they will never want to click on it. Therefore, there are some tried and true methods that you can use to entice them to want to click."

He went to the whiteboard and jotted this down:

- What Is the Text on the CTA?
- Where Should the CTA Be on the Page?
- What Is the Hierarchy of CTAs?
- What Pages Should Have a CTA?

WHAT IS THE TEXT ON THE CTA?

"The text on your CTA shouldn't be weak or vague," he said, capping his marker once more. "Nor should you command a potential client to do something; just like a teenager, no one wants to be told what to do. Therefore, don't use the default text, which is often 'submit' on any buttons."

"Here are a few examples of weak or vague CTAs:

- Click Here
- Contact Us
- Learn More
- Our Process
- Our Services
- Find Out About Us
- Curious?

"Your CTA should generate excitement. Therefore, you need to choose words that elicit emotions. They should also begin with a verb and direct the visitor on what action to take. Here are several examples of action-oriented CTAs:

SENSE OF URGENCY OR SCARCITY

- Biggest Ever
- Don't Miss Out
- Exclusive
- Hurry
- Insider
- Limited / Limited Edition
- Little-Known
- Must End
- Now
- Offer Ends
- One-Off / One-Time
- Unique
- While Supplies Last

GREED

- Cheap
- Exclusive
- Free
- Gift
- More
- Save

SPEED OR LAZINESS

- Easy
- Effortless
- Grab
- Now
- Quick

TRUST

- Authentic
- Expert
- Proven
- Refund
- Secure
- Tested

WHERE SHOULD THE CTA BE ON THE PAGE?

"We want the CTA to stand out and pop off the page, so placement is critical. Studies have shown that people will scan a site in either a 'Z' or 'F' pattern. Therefore, the top right and the middle of your slideshow area are the best two places to place a CTA.

"If you want people to call or contact you, then place the phone number or 'contact us' button in the top right corner," he said confidently.

"Going further down the page, you need to have a clickable element, such as an image or box, that differentiates it from the rest of the page. Also, include plenty of white space around it so that the eye is drawn naturally to it.

WHAT IS THE HIERARCHY OF CTAS?

"Just like a page has a hierarchy, so will your CTAs. As I mentioned before, the top-right will be the "top-dog" CTA, followed by the CTA in your Slideshow Area. However, there may be times when you will need two stacked side-by-side. Here are some basic guidelines for those, as explained by UX designer Oscar Gonzalez:

- When using one button as your primary CTA at the bottom of a section, it should be centered.
- If you have a group of two buttons aligned to the right, the primary button should be on the far right, with the secondary button on the immediate left.
- If you have a group of two buttons aligned to the left, the primary button should be on the far left, with the secondary button to the immediate right. The reason being is for consistency, and hierarchy. Also we read left to right, so having it on the left makes it pop first.

WHAT PAGES SHOULD HAVE A CTA?

"Every page needs one! Obviously, your home page and landing pages should have a CTA, but every other page should have some sort of CTA on it related to the context and subject of the page. You want your potential clients to engage with your content as much as possible."

ONLINE FORMS

"One big issue I see with clients is their forms," Viator said. "You see they want to collect too much information or make it difficult for the user to fill out. Diego Poza of Auth0 said, '86% of users say they quit on registrations because they're too long and too prying.' In his book Influence: The Psychology of Persuasion, Dr. Cialdini wrote, 'The available data have proved him right: Just reducing the number of first-page fields from four to three increases registration completions by 50%.'"

Viator emphasized, "This isn't just for long registration forms either. This goes for any online form. My recommendation is to keep what you collect as limited as possible. You see, your first and last name and email address could be compared to the currency of the web. If I ask you to give me those, what you get in return should be worth it. If I go so far as to ask for more 'personal' information such as phone number(s), location, industry, etc., you may leave saying it's not worth it.

"One other thing I want to say is to have a contact form on your website that simply asks for a person's first name, last name, email address, and message. That is enough information for someone to reach out to you, or for you to follow up with someone later. And for the love of God and all that is holy, don't list your email address on the website in lieu of the contact form."

He then referenced the *Inbound Marketing* book and quoted the authors:

> Using an email address is problematic for three reasons. First, you want to capture your users' contact information in a database in order to nurture these leads should they not be ready to buy just yet; capturing them manually is difficult to do when you're only getting emails from them. Second, you invite spammers who scrape email addresses from websites. And third, people without desktop email applications, such as Outlook, often cannot open those email links. Every contact email address on your site should be replaced with a short web form. Remember, the goal is to make it as easy as possible for the user.

WEB ANALYTICS

"When it comes to your website, understanding your traffic and its sources is crucial," Viator explained. This is where analytics tools come in handy. By incorporating a product like Google Analytics, you can easily track who is visiting your site. You can take it one step further by capturing your prospects' information and identifying more about them with the contact form."

HEAT MAPPING

Viator asked me if I knew what heat mapping was? I told him I didn't have a clue. He said, "Website heat mapping is a way to visually represent user engagement and behavior on a webpage. Most of them will generate a color-coded 'map' that highlights areas of high and low interaction. He went on to say that could go by other names, such as click tracking or click mapping.

"Regardless of what you want to refer to them as, the premise is the same. You are looking at how your site's visitors are interacting with the site.

He then looked over at me, noticing the weight of information that had been imparted, and said, "You look like you're pretty overloaded. I know all this was a lot to take in. Why don't we call it a day, and you can go back to your room, catch some shut-eye, and let your subconscious process everything. We can pick back up tomorrow."

I nodded and stood. "That sounds like a plan." We left together, parted ways at the door of the building, and I headed back to the hotel to get some much-needed sleep.

6 | Blogging for Fun and Profit

It involves an important expenditure. A man interested enough to buy a car will read a volume about it if the volume is interesting.

– Claude Hopkins

Either write something worth reading about or do something worth writing about.

– Ben Franklin

I woke the following day and headed back to The Office Space to catch up with Viator. When I arrived, he wasn't there, so I sat down at the bar and tried to take in everything that he had told me up to this point. I wasn't going to lie, my head was spinning like a record. The more I sat there, the more I tried to process everything, and the more it felt like I was just spinning my wheels.

One of the desk attendants knocked on the doorframe of the conference room. "Hey, I was just going to make a latte. Want one?"

I gladly accepted and stood. "I'll keep you company, if you like."

She smiled, gesturing for me to follow her to the kitchen. "I'm Mae, by the way. "I know you're waiting on Viator, but what brings you here?"

"Well, funny you should say that, as I'm not entirely sure." I told her everything that had happened until that point. When I mentioned any of the encounters with Otto, Constanze, and Phoebus, her pleasant expression was marred with disgust and hatred. I'm pretty sure I also saw daggers leap from her eyes like a middle school teacher calling down some unruly students.

"Stay far away from those jokers. They're nothing but bad news!" She shook her head, as she finished the lattes complete with art. I've seen them drag many small businesses down over the years."

"Really." I frowned. "How so?"

Just as Mae was about to answer, Viator walked in. He greeted me with a handshake and grinned. "Let's get today started."

I thanked Mae for the drink and the conversation and returned to the conference room with Viator. As I sat down, he asked, "Do you know what a blog is?"

"Yeah, I think so. I mean, I have seen them, but I know I don't read them, and I don't think anyone else does either."

"Hmm, so what you are saying is that because you don't do it, that means everyone else doesn't either." The sharpness in his tone warned me I was about to be scolded.

I tried to backpedal, but Viator stopped me cold.

"You see, here you go having the wrong mentality again. Remember when I said your website could be compared to the *Holy Bible* in that people jump in and around in it?"

"Yeah."

"Ok, well, if a user goes to the search engines and looks for something, the likelihood of them sending the searcher to the front page of your website is slimmer based on the number of pages you have on your site. The more content you have, the greater the chance to show on the SERPs. A blog is a great way to help you build trust with prospects and provide an extra level of customer service for your existing clients. It's also a great tool for generating new content for SEO and social media."

"Wait." I put up a hand to halt him and blinked a few times. "I thought blogs were for guys in their parent's basements writing about conspiracy theories or like someone's personal journal for all the world to read. But what you are saying is they are actually useful for small businesses like mine?"

"Yes, seven times seventy, yes!" Viator exclaimed. "You can call it a blog, articles, news, or fishing report if you want. It doesn't matter what it's called as long as it makes sense in the grand scheme of your website. You want to publish content consistently, and that shows the search engines you are the expert in your area."

He went on to explain that in late 2022, Google announced an update to their Quality Rater Guidelines (QRG) that added an extra E for Experience to the preexisting E-A-T guideline (E-E-A-T). E-A-T stood for Expertise, Authoritativeness, and Trustworthiness."[1, 2, 3]

The guidelines now look for:

- **E**: How experienced you are with a topic(s)
- **E**: Your expertise on the topic(s)
- **A**: How authoritative you are about the topic(s)
- **T**: Your general level of trustworthiness

"You see, Google's mission—and really that of any search engines—is to help organize information and make it easily accessible and useful for everyone. Or, as Google put it in their blog post about the E-E-A-T update, they're 'by no means abandoning the fundamental principle that Search seeks to surface reliable information, especially on topics where information quality is critically important. Rather, [they] hope these updates better capture the nuances of how people look for information and the diversity of quality information that exists in the world.'"[4]

Viator leaned back in his chair. "A blog is by far the simplest approach to develop SEO content. In other words, don't think about a blog as something someone will read and consume every time you post; the harsh reality is that the average small business's blog is not likely to develop a cult following. You need to think of and treat the blog as a place where you can show your thought leadership and expertise. By doing so, it is automatically search engine friendly.

"One last thing before I get into more details for what to blog about and how to present it: you need to realize that a blog is a key component of marketing your rural business, and it gives you plenty of content to use in social media posts and email newsletters. Is all that making sense?"

- It follows a content plan and has a cadence to the posting
- You need to post on your website
- Helps to support your small business
- Increases E-E-A-T
- Helps generate content for social media and email newstters
- Generates traffic to your site and is a great place for SEO content
- Answers Searchers Questions

"Yes," I said with a sense of clarity. "It all makes so much more sense now."

"Great, now let's get a few housekeeping-type things out of the way regarding blogging," Viator said, making his way to the whiteboard again. He proceeded to list these items:

- Follow a content plan and have a cadence to the posting
- Post on your website
- Helps to support your small business
- Increases E-E-A-T
- Helps generate content for social media and email newsletters
- Generates traffic to your site and is a great place for SEO content
- Answers searchers questions

CONTENT PLAN AND CADENCE

"For a blog to be effective," Viator explained, "you must follow a content plan. You also have to have a cadence to the posting. Every time the search engines send out their web spiders, they look for new content. If they realize you are posting two times a month, they will come back and crawl it more often.

"Another thing to consider is whether your competition is blogging. What I have found most often is that for the rural small business competing against fellow rural small businesses, chances are they aren't doing much, if anything. If you are going up against a regional competition or chain, then your task will be harder but not impossible to compete; you just have to make sure your blog is better.

"Lastly, at a minimum, you need to be posting once a month to be effective. Posting once a week for three weeks, then stopping for five weeks, then pushing out seven posts in a month isn't going to help you at all. That goes back to the cadence and the search engine spiders crawling your site. If you have enough to say, you could post bi-monthly, weekly, bi- or tri-weekly, or even daily."

KEEP THE BLOG ON YOUR WEBSITE

"If you recall, I quoted Joe Pulizzi about not building your business on rented land. The same goes for your blog. Back in the early late 1990s and early 2000s, blogging was first starting to become mainstream. There were free sites like Xanga, LiveJournal, and Blogger where you could post to your heart's content. But just like social media, it is your blog, your expertise on someone else's site."

David Meerman Scott says it best in his book, *The New Rules of Marketing & PR*, that for "long-term marketing success for your business and your personal brand, you need a blog or similar permanent content site that you own and control."[5]

A BLOG HELPS TO SUPPORT
YOUR RURAL SMALL BUSINESS

"We have already talked extensively about your website, but what bears repeating is that it's your most valuable marketing asset," Viator said, his voice brimming with conviction. "It allows you to tell your full story and craft your message in your own words."

"But don't take my word for it," he said as he pulled a folded piece of paper from his pocket. It was titled "Top Ten Blogging Statistics" and said the following:

1. Blog posts of 2,000 or more words are far
    more likely to have better results.[6]
2. Websites with a blog have almost 4.5
    times more indexed pages.[7]
3. Seven out of ten bloggers say graphics are an
    important aspect of their marketing strategy.[8]
4. Blogging helps companies get 97%

more links to their website.[9]

5. Blogs have been rated as the 5th most trustworthy
    source for gathering online information.10

6. SEO leads have nearly a 3 out of 20 close
    rate, while outbound leads have less than a
    little over 1 out of 100 close rate.11

7. Nine out of ten articles with images receive
    more views than those without them.[12]

8. Using photos of real people instead of stock photos
    can result in a 35% conversion increase.13

9. Marketers who prioritize blogging are 13 times
    more likely to see a good ROI on their efforts.[14]

10. Nearly six out of ten marketers say they've gained
    clients specifically through blogging.[15]

INCREASES E-E-A-T

"Now, I know I mentioned E-A-T and E-E-A-T earlier, but let's dive a little deeper into it. As you know, E-A-T stands for Expertise, Authority, and Trustworthiness and is what Google was looking for as part of their QRG back before December of 2022. Now they have added the extra E to it, which stands for experience.

"Lily Ray of Search Engine Journal says, 'The addition of 'experience' indicates that content quality can also be evaluated through the lens of understanding the extent to which the content creator has first-hand experience in the topic.'[16] Or in other words, Google not only wants to see that you are an expert in what you do, but you also have hands-on experience dealing with the topic.

"Let's look at the E-A-T part now," he said with authority, drawing my attention to the crucial topic at hand. "Now, what you might not also know is that the E-A-T guidelines were also part of Google's 'Your Money, Your Life' (YMYL) guidelines. [17] These were pages or topics that Google believes could affect the 'future happiness, health, financial stability or safety of users.' Essentially, the information on that page has the potential to have a significant impact on the searchers' life."

1. Site secured with Secure Socket Layer/SSL 🔒
2. An about page
3. Clear and easy-to-find contact information
4. Up-to-date reviews and testimonials
5. Terms and Conditions and privacy policy pages
6. Author names and bios on blog posts or articles
7. Accurate citations (Google Business Profile, directory listings, and links to social media accounts)
8. Backlinks from authoritative sites

8 QUICK WAYS TO INCREASE AND PROVE TO GOOGLE YOU HAVE E-E-A-T

"Let's be honest; Google is an enigma and likes to be mysterious. To their credit, if they weren't, we as marketers would ruin it like a hurricane at a beach wedding," Viator joked.

"Therefore, Google doesn't provide us with any documentation that explicitly outlines their preferred E-E-A-T signals other than what is in the QRG. But there are some SEO tactics that are widely used to help Google bots."

He then wrote this list on the board:

1. Site secured with a Secure Socket Layer certificate or the SSL certificate
2. An About page
3. Clear and easy-to-find contact information
4. Up-to-date reviews and testimonials
5. Terms and conditions and privacy policy pages
6. Author names and bios on blog posts or articles
7. Accurate citations (Google Business Profile, directory listings, and links to your social media accounts)
8. Backlinks from authoritative sites

HELPS GENERATE CONTENT FOR SOCIAL MEDIA AND EMAIL NEWSLETTERS

"If you are consistently blogging, then you will have a steady stream of content you can use in your social media post and your email marketing." he declared, his words carrying the weight of undeniable truth. "If you write a 2,000-word blog post, you should be able to pull at least 3-5 quotes from it to use on social media, in addition to the share of the post itself.

"With your email marketing, you could share the top blogs for the month with the first few paragraphs and then include link to the rest of the post. Or you may want to let the blog take up the majority of your email, with a link for readers to follow to your website for the rest of the story."

GENERATES TRAFFIC TO YOUR SITE AND IS A GREAT PLACE FOR SEO CONTENT

Viator's voice reverberated with unwavering conviction as he leaned in, his eyes ablaze with purpose. "Listen closely," he declared, his words resonating with profound significance. "Whether your traffic emanates from the mighty realms of Google, the vibrant corridors of social media, the personalized touch of email marketing, or the interconnected web of links, blogging unveils a multitude of paths through which potential clients can discover your website and engage with your small business." The weight of his statement lingered in the air, underscoring the transformative power that lay within the art of blogging, and the countless opportunities it held to connect, captivate, and cultivate relationships with a diverse array of prospective clients.

"Listen closely," Viator declared, his words resonating with profound significance. "Whether your traffic comes from Google, social media, email marketing, or links, blogging provides several paths by which potential clients can find your website and interact with your small business.

"To quote David Ogilvy, 'Every advertisement should be thought of as a contribution to the complex symbol which is the brand image.' So think about it like this: if you replaced 'blog post' and 'rural' in that sentence, you would have, 'every blog post should be thought of as a contribution to the complex symbol which is your rural business.' Do you understand how a blog can help you more now?"

"Yeah, I think I do. It has certainly been an eye-opening experience for sure."

ANSWERS SEARCHERS QUESTIONS

"Good, very good," he said. "Now, let's look at some things you need to do with your blog to make it more attractive to the search engines, searchers, and prospects."

"The best thing you can do through your blog is to answer peoples' questions," he said with the authority of a Southern Baptist preacher preaching a revival. "You see, search engines are places where we go to do searches, but what else do you think they could be called?"

I looked at him with a puzzled look on my face.

"Ok, think about this. What do you do when you have a question, or you are curious about what else some actor or actress played when watching a movie or TV."

"I go to Google and search for it," I said.

"Exactly. You see, search engines could also be called 'curiosity answerers' because when we're curious about something, we go to them to find the answers. Therefore, your website needs to be there to answer questions related to your business.

"You see now why I say one of the number one reasons you should be blogging is to have a platform where you can answer all the questions you are normally asked on a day-to-day basis. Think about how nice it would be to talk to someone who has done all their research, knows everything about your business, and ultimately what they want?"

That could be helpful," I said with a touch of excitement in my voice. "It would certainly help me have more time."

5 THINGS YOU NEED TO DO ON YOUR BLOG POST

1. USE LAYMAN'S TERMS AND THE WORDS YOUR CLIENTS USE

Just like we talked about how to word things on your website copy, you need to do the same on your blog. In other words, use the same words and phrases that your ideal clientele use.

2. BE HUMAN

Many times, people will try to write for the search engines or sound "corporate." Only robots—and "big corporate robots"—want to read that. Google and all the search engines are getting increasingly sophisticated and learning to analyze your content more like a human. Therefore, don't be afraid to put a personal story in if it helps better explain the post's topic.

Kindra Hall writes in her book *Stories That Stick* that:

> …as the data increases and the metrics become more trackable, it's easy to get sucked into the analytics of it all and, in the process, forget that, on the other side of those metrics, is a person.
>
> A person with a problem.
>
> A person who needs you to solve that problem.
>
> A person who needs a story to captivate them, assure them your solution is the right one, and turn them into a believer.
>
> Ignoring what your business offers can seem like heresy for the uninitiated. But doing so does one critical thing: it forces you to focus on the customer. If you can't talk about your product, what's left? Answer: the people using it.[18]

3. USING STORY TO TELL THE DATA

Kindra Hall also says, "People don't buy the thing. They buy what the thing will do for them. In order for them to do that, you have to tell them a story. That story is a value story." [19]

You may have heard the analogy of the drill bit. But here is the thing—you don't buy the drill bit. You buy what the drill bit provides: the hole. But it can be much bigger than that. You are also buying the satisfaction of completing the project to the satisfaction of your significant other or friends and enjoying the recognition and praise they bestow.

4. USE LISTS TO CONVEY INFORMATION

We, as humans, inevitably have a harder time trying to deal with lots of information without first breaking it down. This is why a list makes so much sense. According to the late psychologist Dr. George A. Miller, "the average human mind cannot deal with more than seven units at a time, which is why seven is a popular number for lists that have to be remembered. Seven-digit phone numbers, the seven wonders of the world, seven-card stud, Snow White and the seven dwarfs, the seven danger signals of cancer."[20]

5. KEEP IT LONG ENOUGH TO COVER THE SUBJECT BUT SHORT ENOUGH TO KEEP IT INTERESTING

When it comes to how long your post should be, some will say 2,000 words or more, while some will say 800 words are enough. While there is evidence that longer tends to do better, that isn't to say shorter might work better for your audience.

When I'm asked this question, I quote my senior English teacher, Mrs. Nichols: "It should be like a woman's skirt: long enough to cover the subject but short enough to keep it interesting."

While the analogy might be a bit crude or cringy, as my son would say, the truth is it works. In this digital age, people skim everything, especially online. According to HubSpot, "73% of people admit to skimming blog posts."[21] We scan for the keywords, and we are looking for the answers to our question(s).

Use headlines and bullet points to make it easier, and don't ramble on and on trying to hit a certain number of words. It doesn't do you any favors—not in the eyes of the user or that of Google. The bottom line when it comes to content length is quality over quantity!

Viator cleared his throat and grinned. "Is this clear as mud?"

"No," I said. "I think I better understand the reason for a blog, but I guess my bigger question is more specific. What exactly should I blog about? I know you mentioned answering people's questions."

"That is an excellent question!" his voice brimming with enthusiasm. "We can talk about it now, or we can call it a day. It's your choice."

I thought for a moment, stood, and stretched. Then I nodded toward the door. "Let's get a bit to eat, and I think I will be good."

With that, we headed down the street for some grub.

7 | They Ask, You Answer

As we exited The Office Space, Viator gestured with his thumb. "The restaurant is just a jump down the street." He had his phone out and looked like he was texting someone. I didn't think much of it, as he was free to do as he wished.

Hardly looking up from his phone as we walked, Viator led me across the busy street. "The restaurant I wanted to take you to is called 'Sweet Chick of Mine.' It's a great BBQ chicken joint, and they have a good variety of other things."

We walked up and the façade welcomed patrons with bursts of colors, mixed with black and chrome. There was also a chicken statue to the right painted with the look of a black leather jacket and chrome studs. On the left was a large neon sign that proudly displayed the name "Sweet Chick of Mine" in bold, flashy letters. The sign illuminated the surroundings with a warm glow.

As we entered, I took a look around. Now, I had been in plenty of BBQ restaurants in my time, but nothing like this. The entire restaurant was decorated with a chicken theme matching the front. There must have been fifty chickens all decked in distinctly '80s heavy metal attire. There were paintings of famous albums and bands from the era, but instead of the artists, chickens posed in the album cover outfits. Even the music playing from the ceiling speakers fit the theme, but the owner had clearly chosen the instrumental versions so as not to impede patron's conversations.

The tables had brushed metal tops outlined in bright chrome. The chairs, barstools, and booth seats were covered in black vinyl and edged with hammered chrome tacks to complete the rocker vibe.

We were escorted to a table away from most of the other patrons but with a clear view of the door. Then we waited for the waitress to come by and take our drink order.

Viator ordered an additional drink, and I thought he was either really thirsty, someone was joining us, or he was crazy. If I was being honest, my jury was still out on the latter.

While we waited on the drinks, I glanced over the menu. Viator lowered his menu for a moment, and I lowered mine. "You know how I have mentioned David Ogilvy," He said.

"Yeah," I replied.

"Some would argue that he was one of, if not *the*, greatest copywriter in the history of advertising."

I smiled and shook my head in agreement.

He must have sensed my lack of enthusiasm. "You see, Ogilvy was a master of advertising. You see, he once ran a series of ads that didn't advertise or talk about his agency, Ogilvy & Mathers, at all. Instead, the ads detailed exactly how to do what he and his agency did. And I don't mean a high-level version; I mean a detailed series of ads that told folks what to do and shared his company secrets."[1]

"Well," I replied, with a touch of doubt in my voice, "someone as famous and influential as Ogilvy could afford to take those bold steps. But for someone like me, it would be risky and might hurt my business."

Viator leaned in, eager to challenge my view. "You know," he responded, "that's where you're mistaken. Yes, anyone can find articles or videos on how to do things. But the truth is, if they don't have enough time, skills, or expertise, their efforts are likely to fall short and fail."

"Think about the social media meme posts or even the Netflix show Nailed It!, which were inspired by the craze. People try and try to recreate what the experts do and usually fail in the process. But here is the thing: Ogilvy knew it and did it before it was even a thing! See, he was fully aware of the difference that exists between being shown something and actually being able to do it or recreate it." [2]

The bell on the restaurant door jingled as two men walked in. Viator stood and greeted him, and as they sat down, Viator introduced him as Marcus Sheridan, author of several books, the founder and force behind the "They Ask, You Answer" Movement, and Anna Sheppard.

Viator caught them up to speed, then Marcus looked at me and said, "I bet you are still wondering and thinking if all this is going to work. Or that we don't understand that your business is different."

I sheepishly agreed. "Well, if I'm being honest, yes, I still have some doubts. But maybe I'm just optimistically skeptical."

Marcus chuckled and then began to tell a story about the struggles he encountered while running a pool company. On Monday, September 29, 2008, the stock market fell almost 800 points, and over the next two days, they lost five customers who had put down deposits. This equated to approximately $250,000 in losses. By January 2009, they were told to file for bankruptcy. But here's the thing: he wasn't ready to give up.

"In 2007," he recounted, "during a time when home values were inflated and easy credit allowed anyone to buy a swimming pool, we achieved around $4 million in business. However, to attain that level of success, we had to allocate approximately $250,000 towards our advertising and marketing endeavors. In contrast, if you fast-forward to 2014—a time when most swimming pool builders were still dramatically down from the pre-recession time period—we did about $5.5 million in business and spent roughly $20,000 on advertising and marketing. By 2018, revenue exceeded $8 million.[3] In 2022, our estimated revenue was between $16 and $18 million."[4, 5]

The waitress arrived just then with our drinks. We thanked her and then placed our order.

As she hurried off, Marcus folded his hands around his cup. "You see, we've had our ups and downs. But out of the pain of almost going bankrupt, the 'They Ask, You Answer' Movement was born."

I said, "That is great for two, but I just don't know if it will work for my business. Viator seems to think so, but I'm just not sure."

Anna's voice resonated with unwavering confidence as he leaned in. "I know it will because I have seen it firsthand," she declared, her words carrying the weight of experience and success. "We have seen this strategy work wonders across countless businesses and spanning every imaginable industry. And without a doubt, I know it will work for you."

Viator looked me dead in the eye. "Why the doubt all of a sudden? Have you seen, been visited by, or talked to Otto, Constanze, and Phoebus again?"

In unison, Anna and Marcus's voice rang out with a touch of frustration, their tone laced with conviction. "Not those jokers!" they exclaimed, their words filled with a hint of disdain. "All they do is hold you back."

TRUST

Viator interjected before they could say anymore about the trio. "Why don't you elaborate on the 'different' phenomenon?" he suggested.

"Sure." Marcus took a sip from his drink and looked thoughtful. "Y'know, I've spoken all over the world and talked to thousands of people, and during all my talks, I ask, 'How many of you, by show of hands, believe your business is quite different than the rest of those in the room?'"

He met my gaze intently. "What do you think the results are?"

"I don't know," I said, looking down at the table.

"One hundred percent."

My jaw dropped. "Really? Everyone always thinks their business is different than everyone else's?"

"Yes!" Marcus exclaimed, his voice brimming with enthusiasm. "You see, we all want to feel special and believe that our business is special as well."[6]

Nodding, Viator spoke up. "It is all based on trust, and it all comes back to it. Just like I asked you to trust me at the start of all this. Everything is built on trust."

"You're right," Anna said in a calm and collected tone. "The companies that embrace this reality and let go of the obsession that 'we're different' are often the ones doing incredible things in their spaces."[7]

BE A TEACHER, NOT A SALESMAN

The waitress returned and set baskets of steaming-hot barbecued chicken in front of each of us. My mouth watered at the sight, and we began to eat.

After breathing like a dragon for a moment and swallowing a bite of food, Viator took a sip of his drink and said, "To help build trust, you have to think like a teacher."

"Think like a teacher?"

"Yes! You see, my wife is a middle school teacher and one of the top teachers in the state. She was also the teacher of the year for the county one time." Viator beamed proudly, then seemed to remember the context of our conversation. "But I digress. She gets a new crop of kids every school year, and she has to build trust with them. Now, this isn't always easy, and she has had some really good and terrible years. The point is, she puts her heart and soul into trying to build trust with the kids and help those who want to learn.

"So, to tie this together, when you have an educational and teaching mindset around your business's sales and marketing, you build trust. By offering informative and educational content on your website, you are positioning yourself as an expert. With a teaching mindset, you start to build long-term relationships. Then when it comes time to make the sale, it goes much smoother for you and the buyer. The bottom line is, it doesn't matter if you are in sales or if you're marketing your business. The more you can build trust with and teach potential people, the better off you will be."

"That is exactly right," Anna said. "When an organization embraces 'They Ask, You Answer' (or TAYA), they believe it's their duty to be the teacher, the go-to source within their particular industry. One that's not afraid to answer any and every question the prospect or client may have. For them, it's a moral obligation to provide this level of education, regardless of whether the question is perceived as good, bad, or even ugly."[8]

THE SALES SHIFT

Viator said, "Since the mid-to-late '00s, there has been a huge shift in people researching and making a buying decision before contacting the business; a little over 70% of buyers do this. Gartner also reports a generational divide in the skepticism of sales representatives. Gen Xers (those born between the mid-1960s to the early 1980s) were 1.4x more skeptical of sales reps, while Millennials (those born between the mid-1980s to the late 1990s) were 2.2x more skeptical of sales reps.[9]

"I don't see this trend stopping with the Gen Z or Centennials (those born between the late 1990s to 2010), as they don't know life without the Internet, and some barely know life without smartphones and tablets."

"I get what you are saying." I responded, nodding in agreement. "People don't want to talk to a salesperson. They would rather do the research themselves."

"Right," Viator chimed in. "So, if traditional lead generation is about being found, then the search engines are the gateway, correct?"

"Yeah, that makes sense," I said.

Anna leaned forward and addressed me. "Which department has the greatest impact on your business's profit-making? Marketing or sales?"

I thought for a moment. But when I opened my mouth to speak, Anna cut in, "It's marketing," she answered for me.

Ignoring the mildly annoyed stare I gave her, Marcus continued. "You see, Marketing is always the first department to get laid off, and Sales is the first to get hired, but in reality, it should be the opposite. In the past, Sales was always viewed as the revenue driver, and Marketing was the expense. But now, you can't say that."

"You are absolutely right," Viator affirmed, his voice filled with agreement and appreciation for the duo's insight. Pausing briefly, he shifted his gaze towards me, a spark of anticipation in his eyes. "Rural small businesses have a remarkable opportunity to tap into people's inherent desire and need to consume information before taking action," he emphasized. "And this is precisely where the TAYA model comes into play."

FIVE BLOG TOPICS THAT WILL DRIVE TRAFFIC, LEADS, & SALES

Viator continued saying that, "In September 2019, before Covid rocked the world, I went to a conference in Boston. In preparation for the trip, I knew I would be changing planes and walking through the city. Being the fish out of water that I am in a big city like that, the last thing I wanted to do was look like more of a tourist than I already was. I also knew I didn't want to take the family luggage and try to wheel it down the sidewalk. So I started researching luggage and bags.

"Here were my criteria:

- I wanted something I would wear, like a backpack.
- It had to have good handles, as I didn't want it breaking while crossing the road.
- I wanted one that I could also carry like a briefcase.
- It had to have good shoulder straps.
- It had to fit in an overhead compartment on the plane.
- A waist belt would be a nice addition.

"I spoke with one of my closest friends, Dana. To say he is a globe trotter is an understatement. Anytime I need advice on travel, he's my go-to! He recommended one that he loved at the time, the 'Rick Steves Convertible Carry-On.' I think he was on his second one in 30 years.

"But even though he gave me a solid recommendation, I still wanted to do my own research. So I went down the rabbit hole (aka the buyer's journey/research) into the bag. I looked at the reviews, 'best of' lists, and comparison videos discussing problems, pros, and cons. I also compared the cost of this bag to others like it on the market."

Viator's voice grew more intense as he continued, "If I did all this for a $100 backpack, do you think your clients are doing the same for your services?"

I thought for a moment, but before I could answer, Viator cut me off. "Yes! At least seven out of ten of them are!"

Marcus spoke up again, nodding. "You see, there are five major topics that any business needs to address on their website."

1. Problems
2. Comparisons
3. "Best of" Lists
4. Social Proof
5. Cost

1. PROBLEMS

Marcus continued, "The first one you need to talk about is problems—the searchers/buyers' problems and your problems."

My brow furrowed. Why would I want to talk about problems? That seemed like a negative way to start a business relationship.

Viator grinned looking at the expression on my face. "I know you think we're crazy. But think about this: are your competitors doing it? Is everyone asking about the problems? If the answer is yes to either of those, you have to be prepared to talk about it!"

Marcus said, "You are exactly right. You see, when people buy, they worry more about what might go wrong than about what will go right."[10]

"Marcus, you are exactly right. Let me give you an example, still using the backpack," Viator said. "When I bought the backpack, I went to Google and typed in 'Rick Steves Convertible Carry-On reviews.' I refined the search even more, using terms and phrases that could be deemed negative. If I was going to throw down the money for the bag, I wanted to make sure it would be what I needed and wanted—the good, the bad, and the ugly, if you will."

"Now, back when I was just a pool guy," Marcus said, "one of the biggest questions I got was, 'What are the problems with a fiberglass swimming pool?' And I would always dance around it, afraid to be honest and transparent. But when I embraced the TAYA philosophy, we addressed it directly on the website. I'm also happy to share that one post about fiberglass swimming pools has generated over one million dollars in revenue."

Viator elaborated further, "It goes back to trust and transparency. By addressing what none of your competitors wants to talk about but everyone is asking, you can only benefit.

"When you talk about problems, you need to address the prospects' problems and your problems. Prospects may only know the symptoms of their problems and may not have any clue you have the solution. If you want to help them solve said problems, you have to show up with the answers. To show up, you have to have content that addresses the symptoms and let them know the options for solving them. You also need to talk about problems with your solution.

"For example, let's say a prospect is having trouble with a water heater. They start their journey searching for 'why is my water heater not working,' and they discover their old water heater is probably shot. Then they educate themselves about the different types of water heating systems: conventional storage-tank water heater, tankless water heater, hybrid water heater, or solar-powered water heater. They will most likely do just as I did and start looking for positive and negative reviews, as well as for potential problems with the different solutions."

Anna popped the last piece of chicken into her mouth and said, "The most effective way to immediately show you're unbiased is by discussing who your product or service is *not* for."

Viator nodded. "It can be a tough pill to swallow that your solution isn't right for them. But would you rather address it on your website or have to hold that in-person meeting and break the news that you don't offer what they want, or that what they have their heart set on won't work for them and their situation? In other words, be honest and think of all that research they can do without you as a way to weed out the bad fits."

2. COMPARISONS

Viator's voice carried a sense of importance as he continued, "Comparisons are the next on the list, and they are one of the most important pieces of content you can create. They are also one of the hardest. When comparing products or services, prospects are in the final stages of the buyer's journey. The last thing they want is buyer's remorse! Who do you think wants to make a wrong decision?"

"No one," I said, "especially if it's costly!"

"Exactly," he said, his voice resonating with assurance. "Therefore, you have a golden opportunity to talk about all the options with your products or services, how they compare in different categories, the pros and cons of each, and which ones are better under different circumstances. Having an article on your website that honestly compares your product to your competition in detail will build trust."

3. "BEST OF" LISTS

Anna finished her drink with a loud slurp. "What was the last major purchase you made? Did you research it?"

I thought about it. I thought about how big an investment it was and how much research I put into it.

"I bet that as part of that research, you might have looked for a 'Best Of' list—'Top Five,' 'Top Ten,' or something to that effect." Anna remarked. "Regardless if you did or didn't, those are one of the most common ways people search.

"As the old saying goes, 'Build a better mousetrap, and the world will beat a path to your door.' This isn't because they want a better mousetrap. It's because they want a piece of your market share and will ultimately be your competition."

She went on to say that even if I was in a super niche market, I have competitors. Now, these may be actual businesses, or they could be:

> **Status quo Bias** is the desire for things to remain the same. According to Matthew Dixion and Ted McKenna, authors of *The Jolt Effect,* "decades of research in the fields of cognitive psychology and behavioral economics—and the experiences of sellers in every market and industry the world over—teach us that this bias has a tremendous hold on us as human beings. In fact, researchers have found that people will opt for the status quo even when presented with options that entail low switching costs and would clearly make them better off."[11]

> **Commission Bias** is the fear of doing something wrong and the weight of that loss. In other words, everyone wants to avoid loss, "but what they really want to avoid is loss that is the direct result of an action they took."[12]

> **Omission Bias** is when the loss is a result of someone failing to do something. "Simply put, this bias means that people actually

feel more regret when bad things are a result of their actions as opposed to when bad things happen as a result of their inactions."[13] "The omission bias helps explain why a customer who states their intent to abandon the status quo may still end up in a state of indecision, worrying over whether to take action."[14]

Anna nodded, acknowledging my initial resistance. "I understand your concern," she replied. "But here's the thing, for both tangible and intangible competitors, you need to talk about them on the site."

"Talk about them on the website? Why would I want to mention my competitors on the website?" I said both inquisitively and with borderline angry disgust in my voice. "That defeats the purpose! If I do that, it will just tell visitors on my website they should go to the competitors."

Anna could see I was hot about this topic and held up her hands placatingly. "You make valid points, and I know it seems counter-intuitive, but it's really not."

With obvious skepticism in my voice, I said, "How so?"

"If you talk about or list your competitors on your website and someone finds that list, it just means your site is doing its job and putting you above your competition," he said swiftly and confidently. "The bottom line is this: your prospects are smart and informed. If you treat them with respect and honesty, they will appreciate you and your company. If you are the only business willing to address the elephant in the room, you'll get major brownie points."

4. SOCIAL PROOF

Viator went on to explain that social proof comes in many forms, and these are typically user-generated content (UGC). These include reviews and testimonials. Testimonials will come in a variety of forms, such as quotes or case studies. Testimonials will highlight how great or successful users were by using your products or services. Reviews are similar because a good review can move you to the top of the list.

"Going back to my search for a good carry-on bag," Viator said. "In the process of my research, I found through the reviews that people said the backpack straps lacked padding and recommended another bag. I ultimately went with the other bag, as padded straps were critical for me.

"At the time, I had known Dana for fifteen years (more than that now), and I took the words of strangers over one of my best friends whom I had known for years!"

5. COST

"Cost is one the biggest things that needs to be addressed on your website." Viator asserted, his voice filled with conviction.

"I can't do that," I blurted.

Viator was hot on my heels. "I knew you were going to say that. I have heard every excuse in the book. I bet you were going to say one of these:

- My competitors will know how much I charge.
- It might scare people away before I can explain the reasons.
- It depends on the size of the job or how bad it is.
- It depends on too many factors.
- We are a "value-based business."

"All those are just what I said—excuses. Think about this: when you were researching your last big purchase, at any point did you look for pricing? If you are like 999 out of 1000 people, you did. At any point, if you didn't find pricing, did you say, 'Oh, this company is value-based, or there are too many factors for them to give me a price. I will just call them.' Chances are, you moved on to the next business.

"So think about this, how did those companies make you feel? Did they build or erode your trust? Were you frustrated by the process?"

Viator said, "If you don't want to address pricing specifically, then at least give people a range. Tell them it starts at $1,000 and could go to $10,000. While that is a huge range and should maybe be narrowed down, you at least gave them a range." His words carried a sense of urgency and practicality.

"If I haven't convinced you by now, I want you to realize that every time you choose not to address something, you are not being transparent, and you are adding frustration and friction to the process."

"Frustration is a dirty word in my book," Anna spoke up and said. "It is also the F-word of the Internet!"

"A close second is friction," Viator chimed in.

Marcus and Anna both agreed with a hearty nod.

Viator continued. "If you can remove frustration or friction or both from any step in the process, you are ahead of the game. If you can build trust while doing it, then the rest of your job is easy.

"Think about Amazon. They sell some of the same things that the big box stores sell. But unlike the big box store, they make it easy by removing the frustration and the friction. Want to purchase this in one click? Done. Want it in two days? Done. Want to get this without the plastic wrap that doubles as a knife you could field dress an animal with? Done."

"That is something to think about for sure," I responded, a contemplative tone coloring my voice.

We finished up the meal, and I thanked Marcus and Anna for their time as we stood from the table.

Now with a full belly, Viator and I walked back to The Office Space to discuss what else I needed to be doing.

8 | Service, Landing and Geo-Landing Pages, Oh My!

I actually don't think you can sell professional services. I think you have to help clients buy them. Clients have problems and they need help in discovering, understanding, and tackling them. Once people realize you helped them solve problems, then they will come back.

— *Walt Shill*

We walked in silence back from the restaurant. I'm not sure if that was on purpose or not. It allowed me to process what Marcus and Viator told me.

Back at The Office Space, I plopped into a chair at the conference table with a groan.

Viator sat beside me and asked, "What are you thinking?"

"I'm thinking about how stuffed I am," I said.

We laughed, and Viator clapped me on the shoulder. "Are you familiar with a mind map?"

"No, not really."

"No worries, let's start there." He then went to the whiteboard and began to draw a circle with lines coming out of it, much like how a child would draw the sun.

"This drawing represents a mind map, or a way of dumping your brain out on paper—or on a whiteboard—so you can visualize how everything relates to one another. Make sense?"

I nodded in agreement.

"Good. Now, for our purposes, we are going to simplify it a bit into what is referred to as a hub and spoke. Think about a wagon wheel. You have the center part of the hub. Then you have the spokes that come out from the center, or in our case, they go into the center."

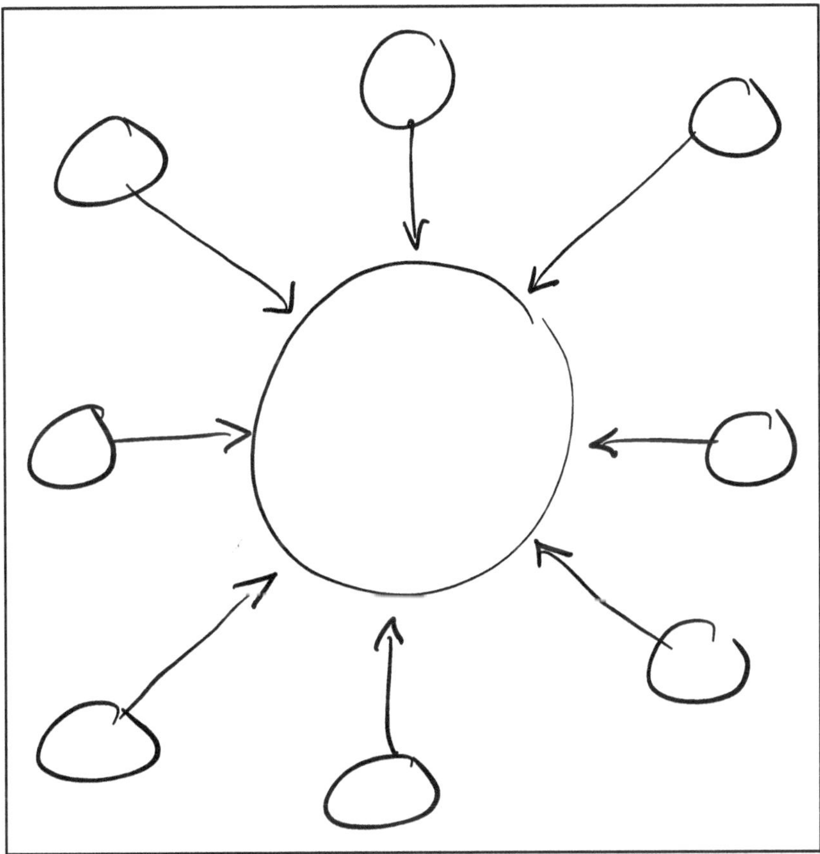

He added some quick strokes that turned the spokes of the wheel into arrows pointing to the center hub. At the other end of each spoke he drew a smaller circle.

Pointing to the center circle, he said, "This is your main service page, and all the spokes are links from around your site pointing into it. The smaller circles represent your blogs and other landing pages. You can have links from the blogs or other landing pages pointing in, directing the traffic to your main service page."

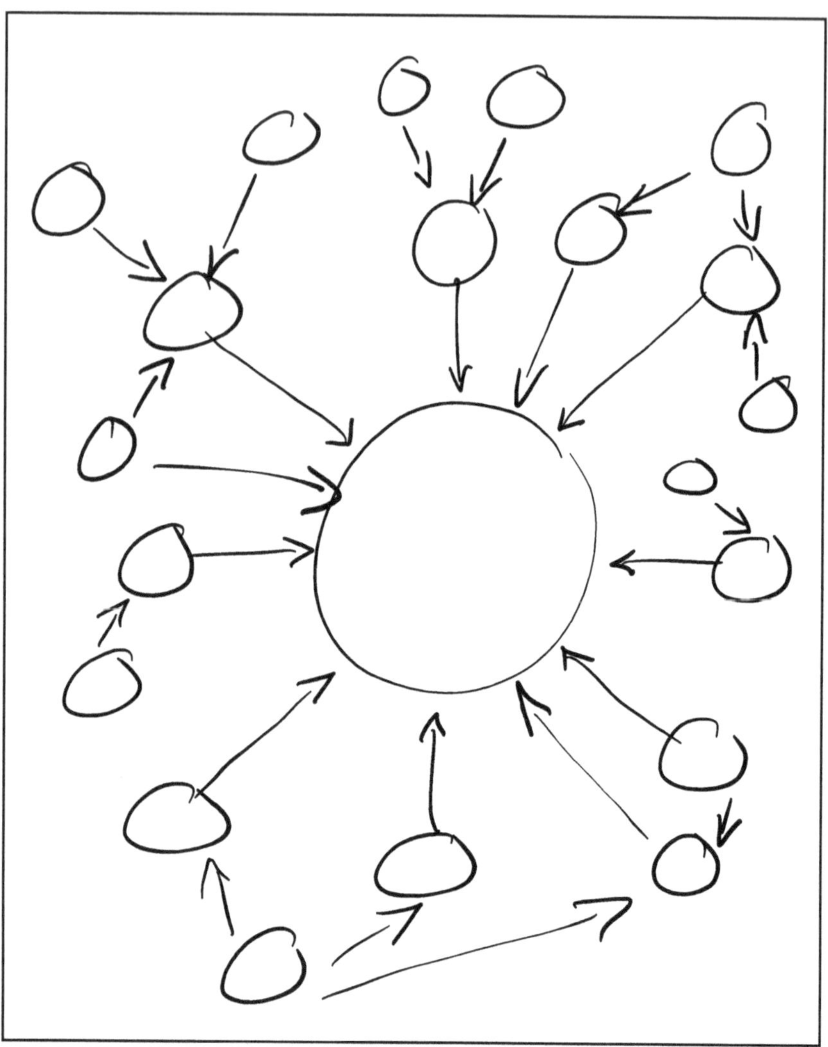

He then started to draw more circles and spokes, connecting them all together.

"Now, recall how I explained how a searcher will come to your website."

"Yes," I said. "You said that searchers may come to a landing page, then jump to another page and another."

"Exactly," he said with a big smile. "If a searcher comes to a landing page as part of their search process, we want to be able to give them a way to find more related information, so we send them to the main hub. These main hubs are going to be deep dives, covering all aspects of the service(s) you offer."

Still standing by the board, Viator asked me, "Do you think we need to cover the service pages, or do you think you have a grasp on that based on what we discussed about how we build the website pages."

I leaned forward in my chair and said, "I think I have a grasp on that, but tell me how landing pages come into play."

Viator went on to explain that Seth Godin, a world-famous author of over 37 marketing books, believes a landing page can and should only make a user take one of five actions[1]

1. Get a visitor to click (to go to another page, on your site or someone else's)
2. Get a visitor to buy
3. Get a visitor to give permission for you to follow up (by email, phone, etc.). This includes registration, of course
4. Get a visitor to tell a friend
5. Get a visitor to learn something, which could even include posting a comment or giving you some sort of feedback

Viator interjected with an additional insight, "One quick additional note," emphasizing the key characteristics of a landing page. "A landing page may or may not have a menu or navigation. It has to be super clean and focus on one topic or one keyword phrase."

TYPES OF LANDING PAGES

"For our purposes, there are three types of landing pages outside of the normal service pages:

- Search Engine Optimized (SEO) Landing Pages
- Local or Geographical Landing Pages
- Marketing, Social, or PPC Landing Pages

"Let's first talk a bit about SEO landing pages. As the name implies, these will be highly optimized for search engines and searchers, or what Google calls 'user intent or searcher intent.' You see, Google wants to serve the most relevant content for what a searcher is looking for. This is where an SEO landing page can help; if your page is there and does the best job of answering the question determined by the algorithm, your page will show up at the top of the SERPs! An SEO landing page should focus on one keyword or keyword phrase.

"The next on our list is the geographic landing page. These also go by other names, such as geo-landing or local landing pages, as they are sometimes called. These are variations of an SEO landing page, but as the name implies, they include a geographical location. They are designed for local search or when a user searches for the keyword or phrase in combination with the 'near me,' 'city,' or zip code determined by Google. More on these in a bit.

"Lastly, you have the marketing, social, or PPC landing pages. These will be used in conjunction with some type of campaign, like an email campaign, social and/or pay-per-click ad, or display ad. For example, if we have a PPC ad, we can point the CTA on the ad to a dedicated landing page where it has similar verbiage as the ad and is focused on converting the visitor.

"The bottom line with all these pages is that your goal is to get the visitor to do something. If you have done your job and provided value, there is a good chance you can help turn that visitor into a lead. Brian Halligan and Dharmesh Shah say, 'A good landing page can convert 50%of its visitors into qualified leads while a poor one will convert less than 1%. Using landing page practices can dramatically improve your conversion rates and lower your cost per lead.'"[2]

LANDING PAGE TIPS

Viator sat back down and said, "Let me share a few additional landing page tips with you.

"When you develop a landing page, make sure you match the content and CTA of your ad, email, etc., to that of your landing pages. The bottom line is this: you don't want prospects to think you are using clickbait tactics.

"This brings me to my next point, which is trust. Everything should be based on trust! If you want to get people to convert on your pages, you need to have a well-designed landing page, including well-written content or copy, images, and overall design that conveys trust.

"I mentioned this before, but if you are doing an email or paid ad of any type, the last thing you want is to send someone to a page that has a menu on it—or, even worse, your social media icons are prominent. That effectively loses them. You spent your hard-earned money on that campaign, and it would be a waste for them to come to that page, bounce to another, or click on your social media, where they get sucked in for two hours and forget what they were doing, to begin with."

Viator gestured with a sweeping motion, emphasizing his point "Piggybacking on that same topic, you need to keep the page clean and simple.

"Remember what I said the other day about forms? Keep them short and only ask for the bare minimum of your needs. Also, don't use the form to ask something the visitor has to go look up.

"Address how you plan to use their email address. Since the age of data breaches and blatant misusage of consumer data, such as in the Cambridge Analytica Scandal, users are much more conscious of how their contact information will be used. Therefore, be transparent and tell the prospect what you will do with the data. You can hire a lawyer to do it and put it in what I call 'lawyery speak,' or just say what you plan to do with it in plain English. Does all that make sense to you?

"Sure does," I said.

Viator leaned forward, "Great, now, let me expand on the geo-pages a bit more because that is where I have seen businesses in rural areas get helped the most." He leaned back, ready to delve into the details, eager to share his insights.

"Great," he said, acknowledging my understanding and his tone brimming with excitement. "Now let me expand on the geo-pages a bit more because that is where I have seen businesses in rural areas get helped the most.

"In a rural area, we have a community just like our urban counterparts; however, our community is geographically much larger.

"Your typical rural small business used to be able to start a business, hang their sign out by the door, or stick a few magnets on their vehicle and start getting phone calls. They then might expand to joining the local Chamber of Commerce and getting involved with local civic organizations and associations. They might also volunteer at schools or the fire department to help get their name out.

"While I'm not discounting those methods, as I believe they still work, these days you have to go beyond that. Today's buyers will Google you in a heartbeat, and if you aren't there to show up, you lose their business before you even had a chance to earn it."

"If you have a small presence, you might be lucky enough to get a phone call, or they might start checking your reviews, or maybe, just maybe, asking about you. When it comes to the rural small businesses I have helped in the past, a good geographic landing page has helped them as much as anything else we have done."

"A geographical landing page has to be unique for each location you are targeting and talk about one service you offer. The service will form part of our top level keywords or phrases for the page. Now what are three of the basic services and three of the areas you cover?"

I told him, and he scribbled them on the board. He then proceeded to brainstorm nine possible landing pages.

He said, "We can take these nine pages, build them out using the modified *Building A Storybrand* framework, created by Donald Miller, and you have nine more chances to rank on the SERPs. You can use the same services, change locations, and get even more!"

"What is the modified *Building A Storybrand* framework?" I asked.

- Section 1: Introduction with headline, sub-head and one call-to-action sentance

- Section 2: Problem or desire around the keyword

- Section 3: Problem the client is facing that the keyword can solve

- Section 4: The solution to the problem you can help solve

- Section 5: A plan to solve the problem

- Section 6: A call-to-action that encourages the next step

> - Section 7: Failure of not taking action
> - Section 8: Success of taking action
> - Section 9: Social Proof / Testimonials
> - Section 10: Why choose your small business
> - Section 11: A call-to-action to get started

"Good question. In the book *Building a StoryBrand: Clarify Your Message So Customers Will Listen*, Donald Miller explains why stories are so important for a brand and a small business like yours. Here is my modified version of it." Turning back to the board, he began to write the following:

- **Section 1**: Introduction with a headline, sub-headline, and one call-to-action sentence
- **Section 2**: The problem or desire the reader may be dealing with, centered around a keyword
- **Section 3**: A problem the prospect is facing that the keyword can solve
- **Section 4**: A solution to the problem that your business can help solve

- **Section 5**: A plan outlining the steps the prospective client needs to take to solve the problem
- **Section 6**: A call to action encouraging the prospect to take the next step
- **Section 7**: A failure, which highlights the consequences of not taking action
- **Section 8**: A success, which shows the positive outcome the prospective client can achieve by taking action
- **Section 9**: Testimonials and Social Proof
- **Section 10**: Why your business
- **Section 11**: A call to action to get started today

"Okay, first things first, each one of these sections will likely need one to three paragraphs and possibly an accompanying visual, like an image." He then proceeded to explain each section.

Section 1 is designed to grab the reader's attention with a powerful headline and sub-head that clearly communicates your business's value proposition. The call-to-action sentence is used to encourage the reader to take action. This will also be one of the first things readers see, so make it powerful and make it memorable.

Section 2 is used to highlight the problem or desire the reader may be experiencing in relation to the service being offered. The goal here is to create a connection with the reader by identifying a problem or desire that they can relate to. This helps to build trust and establish your business as the authority in solving the problem or fulfilling the desire. Once they feel understood and connected with you, they are more likely to continue reading and engaging with the brand. It is also critical for creating an emotional connection with the reader and setting the stage. By identifying the problem or desire, you can transition to offering a solution and outlining the steps readers need to take to solve their problem or fulfill their desire.

Section 3 identifies problems they are facing that the keyword(s) can solve. The goal is to make the reader understand the service's value and how it can help them solve a specific problem. By clearly identifying the problem and showing them how the service you offer can solve it, you further establish yourself as the authority in the industry and build trust with them. You need to keep it clear and concise, avoid technical jargon, etc. This might be the first time the reader is coming across your content, so speak to them that way.

Section 4 introduces the reader to the service offered by your business and how it can solve the problem outlined in Section 3. Overall, this part is critical for presenting the service as the solution to the reader's problem and demonstrating its value and relevance.

Section 5 outlines the steps the reader needs to take to solve the problem and achieve their desired outcome. You may also want to think about this as "The Plan Section." This section is important because it helps the reader understand the process of working with the business and what they can expect from the experience.

I know I mentioned it before, but during the 1960s and 1970s, David Ogilvy ran a series of "house ads" in which they explained exactly how to create an ad as they did. He is quoted as saying:

> Left alone, copywriters write ads to impress other copywriters, and art directors make layouts to impress other art directors.
>
> The purpose of my ads was to project the agency as knowing more about advertising. You may argue that this strategy was ill-advised, knowledge being no guarantee of "creativity." But at least it was unique, because no other agency could have run such advertisements—they lacked the required knowledge.
>
> My ads not only promised useful information, they provided it.[3]

The reason I quote that is so that you realize it's okay to tell people the secret ingredient to your sauce is salt because, the thing is, the people you want to work with won't go to the trouble of creating your sauce. It's easier to let you do it.

Section 6 encourages the reader to take action and engage with the business in some way, whether it's making a purchase, signing up for a newsletter, or scheduling a consultation. The language used in the call-to-action should be direct and action-oriented, using verbs that encourage the reader to act. It should also be presented in a prominent location and stand out visually, such as a brightly-colored button or link.

You may also want the call-to-action to help create a sense of urgency and motivate the reader to act sooner rather than later. This could be done through limited-time offers, discounts, or other incentives.

Section 7 highlights the consequences of not acting and addressing the problem or desire presented in the earlier sections. Here you want to help the reader to understand the potential negative outcomes of inaction, creating a sense of urgency and motivation to take action.

Present the negative consequences of not solving the problem or fulfilling the desire presented in earlier sections. The language used should be direct and descriptive, using vivid imagery and language to create emotional impact within the reader. Additionally, you can differentiate your business from your competitors by highlighting the specific risks or negative outcomes that are unique to the service being offered.

Section 8 shows the reader the positive outcome they can achieve by taking action and engaging with your business. This helps the reader understand the benefits and value they can gain from working with the business, creating a sense of motivation and optimism. You should use descriptive and emotionally resonant language as well as vivid imagery that creates a positive impact on the reader.

Section 9 exists to provide social proof through testimonials and other evidence demonstrating your ability to provide high-quality services. Presenting evidence of previous successes can help the reader feel more confident and motivated to take action and engage with the business.

Section 10 illustrates why the reader should choose you above your competitors. This will help readers understand your unique strengths and advantages and how you can provide value other businesses can't.

Section 11 is the final section and we use it to encourage the reader to take action and get started with the business today.

BONUS SECTIONS

Using a video section can be an effective way to further engage with the reader and communicate the message in a dynamic and compelling way. Video content can be used to provide additional context and information, highlight key benefits and features, and establish a more emotional connection with the reader. They work well as a standalone section with (or in lieu of) section 4 or 9.

Showcasing a geographical location can be an effective approach to personalize the message and strengthen the reader's relationship with your business. By using the reader's geographical location, the business can demonstrate they understand the reader's specific needs and can provide tailored solutions relevant to their location. It also helps the search engines establish your geographical area—which is key if you are a rural business.

ADDITIONAL ITEMS AND INFORMATION TO ADD

Additionally, depending on the context of the section you may want to include the following in each section:

- A call-to-action button should drop them to the bottom of the page for a contact form and contact information.
- An image to help illustrate your point.
- Reference the area, including landmarks such as local, national, and state parks if you need to have the landing page be a mix of marketing and geo.
- If applicable, include pricing as a standalone section for the service(s) you are offering, even if it's a range.
- Consider geotagging your images if possible. Even if it's a cell phone snapshot, it's better than a stock photo that doesn't represent the area.

I held up a hand. "What do you mean by geotagging?"

"A very good question," he said. "A geotagged photo has the GPS data or geographic position embedded in the file. Depending on what you take the photo with, this data may or may not be embedded in it already. Now some think this strategy is a myth, and I can't say for sure either way. But the way I look at it, if the data is there, chances are Google can see and read it. Also, it helps readers know where the image was taken. You have a better chance of increasing your credibility because you were local to their stomping grounds."

"That makes sense, but you mentioned the landmarks. What about businesses and buildings?" I asked, leaning forward in my chair.

"Well, you have to be careful with those. While it might help you with your local people, it won't help with Google. You know as well as I do that those of us in a rural area tend to refer to where the 'old blank was' or 'where the blank used to be.' While we use these as a badge of honor to establish how long we have lived in the area, Google doesn't understand it, nor does it care. So you can mention it, but be careful you aren't relying on just that to help establish where you are.

"One other thing you will want to think about is when you start developing the page, you need to hit up every community you service. Essentially, if they have a zip code, you need to have a series of pages focused around it."

"Yeah, I see your point, but surely Google is smart enough to expand the search radius," I asked.

"Well, yes and no. See, Google, much like your urban counterparts, doesn't understand that we will drive. They think everything needs to be in a three-mile radius."

"Three miles?" I asked.

"Yep. Google released what would become known as the Pigeon Update back on July 25, 2014. While it was designed to help local searchers, Mike Blumenthal determined it reduced the search radius to about three miles, thus effectively hurting rural businesses.[4]

Viator stood up and looked around for his belongings. "I tell you what; let's pack it up here for the day, but there are a couple other people I want you to meet. I reached out to them earlier to see if we could have dinner with them. Thankfully they were available."

Before we exited The Office Space, Viator pulled out his phone and called a car service. The car was ready for us the moment our feet hit the sidewalk, a model just like the one we had ridden in before. As we rode along, I tried to take in all the sights as they whizzed by. It was like a melting pot of all the buildings and places that were there or had been in my town. It was all surreal, but honestly, this whole experience was surreal.

Viator broke the silence. "I hope you like Mediterranean- and Greek-inspired dishes. We're headed to 'For Whom the Gyro Tolls.'"

The look on my face must have said it all as Viator grinned at me. "I think you'll like this place. The owners were big metalheads back in the '80s and '90s, so all the dishes are puns of famous songs from the era."

We arrived at the restaurant to find Viator's two friends waiting for us in the lobby. Viator introduced them as Mike Blumenthal and Carrie Hill. We all shook hands and made our way inside.

As we sat down, Viator asked Mike to fill me in on a bit about his history.

Mike said, "I got started with websites in the early 2000s, and I quickly realized SEO and local SEO were the only ways that the internet made any sense. So I started exploring local SEO in probably 2005, and it became a passion of mine.

"To me, the internet is local, and local is the internet these days. Whether it's e-commerce or social, most businesses are local and have a local component."

Carrie chimed in and said, "I actually started in SEO in 2005. I got hired by a local hospitality marketing company, and I had no background or training in marketing. I live in a fairly small area, and their hiring pool of willing victims was small, so I lucked into a job. And at that job, I met Mary Bowling, and she became my mentor. She took me under her wing and taught me the ways of SEO, and then that naturally progressed into local SEO."

Viator asked Carrie, "Would you mind diving into all the changes you have seen since you started?"

"Sure," she answered. "Back when I started, all you needed were some directory submissions on a webpage to rank on AltaVista, Yahoo, etc. Back then, the index was rebuilt every six weeks, so if you made a change, you waited six weeks, and if it worked great, if not then you you made another change and waited another six weeks. Then around 2012, Google turned the corner and started incorporating knowledge graphs. It was a huge change because local became something that was building upon itself and had memory!"

Mike said, "I take more of a contrarian position because when you look at the Google ranking algorithm, that largely hasn't changed. Certainly, as the web has gotten more sophisticated, and their algorithm has grown with it. But when I go back and look at stuff I wrote, like the '10 Ranking Signals' or 'Google Local in 2007,' what was relevant then is still relevant today. Those being business name, reviews, and citations in the broader sense, links, and website.

"What really changed the most is that Google became a monopoly and really the only power in local SEO. That had tremendous contradictions in it because things like these directories became less valuable and less significant. They sent less and less traffic our way, too. So the big change to me is the market dynamics, not so much what you do to stay on top of it."

Mike leaned forward. "Now, obviously, as Carrie pointed out, Google's changed from re-indexing everything and creating listings every six weeks to a fixed listing. The knowledge graph was a big technical change too, and it certainly fixed a lot of things, like these monster listings we used to see. But to some extent, the activities of an agency and ranking many of the same things that were critical in 2007 are still critical. Again, maybe there are a few more ranking businesses; maybe it's more competitive, maybe there are more web signals. But they were always there; they just weren't as obvious because things were less developed.

"But the beauty of the algorithm has always been its ability to scale from a shoemaker in Kazakhstan to the Plaza Hotel in New York City. The same algorithm ranks that, and it's always done that, and it's always moved from directory listings to website links and everything in between fairly elegantly. Some things stay the same, is all."

"Let me ask you a question, Mike. Viator said you had done some research and found that Google limits searches to about three miles," I asked.

Mike said, "If I recall correctly, that was from my research on storage units. With local search, it's a very dynamic algorithm. Wherever you're searching from physically, wherever they think you are based on your phone's location data, Google will deliver some radius to give you enough relevant results, and that is defined by the portal of the map. That could vary based on industry or population density. So if you're a dentist in New York City, where there's one on every corner, your search results are going to show you locations within even less than three miles. You might only have a quarter mile in any direction from your business before you stop showing.

"If you are in something like an employment lawyer, say, in an area where there aren't many businesses, you might get ten miles radius, so 20-mile diameter. Local search is very dependent, what that means is you have to figure that out. You have to look at how far you want to reach and how far Google will let you reach. If you can do that with local, great, but if you can't, then you have to do it with organic. I think it's a critical calculation to see what Google's delivering in your vertical. In your area, how far are you likely to be visible? Because it varies a lot."

Carrie said, "For me, I'm in a unique area. I live halfway between Vail and Aspen, so I'm 45 minutes from either. There are many businesses in my area that don't market here, but they should. The few businesses that spend the time to build a website put the names of the towns where they want to do business on their website somewhere. Some of them just make a list. Many will use social media groups as well, because they will get on and just answer people's 'in search of' posts, and they stay busy that way."

I tilted my head, considering that. "What would be one tip you would give someone like me?" I asked Carrie.

Carrie chimed in, offering her advice with a thoughtful expression. "My advice would be to put the words on your website that describe what you do. Put what people think you do, too, because that's the vocabulary they use when they describe what you do."

Viator nodded in agreement, adding further clarity to Carrie's point, "To clarify, put things in layman's and slang terms so when someone searches for your business, you have a better chance of being found."

"Right," Carrie said. "And not only do you have to talk about what you do on your website, but you need to have pages about where you do it. You need to answer the questions of what, where, and how. Why should you hire me? When or what's my availability? How do you get a hold of me? How do you book with me? If you can answer those questions with your website in really great fashion, I think you will be set up really well to rank in rural markets.

"Now, the GBP [Google Business Profile] side is another component I think is quite important. It's a great opportunity in a rural market because many people don't do anything with it. Even more, I really think you should start with the GBP in a rural market because organic search is really important."

Mike said, "I agree with Carrie, and I just want to clarify that you have to have one page for each service on your website, as well as pages covering the geography. These extra pages will make your website a little bit bigger, but that's okay."

As the evening progressed, we started discussing everything from life and family, to websites and SEO. You could tell there was a reason Viator wanted me to meet them. Both Mike and Carrie had a mentorship-like attitude that fully enveloped the table.

By the end of the dinner, I felt inspired and had a much better understanding of everything. I expressed my gratitude to the group, recognizing the significance of their guidance and support.

As we left For Whom the Gyro Tolls, Viator buried his nose in his phone again. But before I could comment on my guide's developing antisocial tendencies, he raised his head and met my gaze. "I got you a ride back to your hotel," he said. "As you know, Otto, Constanze, and Phoebus are still out there. You should be fine, though. It's a short ride to your hotel, and I doubt they will try the mirror trick again. I'm actually surprised they used it at all."

Another sleek car slowed to a halt by the sidewalk in front of us. I climbed in, leaning back as Viator reached in and set the destination for me. The doors shut, leaving Viator behind, and I sped back to my hotel.

When the restaurant was just out of sight, the car jostled like it had briefly hit a pothole. The dashboard screen in front of me flickered several times, causing the cabin to be illuminated with a series of rapid flashes of light. I thought nothing of it at first, but then the flashing quickly intensified. The screen went dark. A moment later, I was blinded by its sudden white glow.

A dark shadow appeared on the screen, flickering slightly, and a scratchy digital voice came through the car's speakers. As the car traveled further down the road, the image and voice became clear. It was Phoebus!

Phoebus seemed to see my shock of recognition through the screen, somehow, because he said, "Well, hello again. I know our last encounter was a little unsettling, but I needed to get you alone so we could chat."

I braced myself, expecting a confrontation. But instead of attacking me directly, Phoebus's tone was calm and reasonable.

He said, "I know you think Viator will be able to help you, but are you sure he has his facts right? I will be honest; I'm not sure where he can help you like he says he can. I guess what I'm saying is that he doesn't sound very reliable to me."

"What do you mean by 'reliable'?" I inquired, seeking further clarification on the matter.

Phoebus paused for a moment, contemplating my question before responding. "Consider this," he began, his tone measured and thoughtful. "Have you ever thought of asking him about the number of clients he has lost? I just think you need to better understand his track record before you put all your eggs in his basket."

I began to feel a growing sense of confusion and doubt. Could Phoebus be right? Were Viator, Marcus, Anna, Mike, and Carrie wrong, or was it the other way around? I knew what everyone had been telling me made sense, but I couldn't help but think how coincidental it was that Viator was there when I needed him.

9 | The Social Proof is in the Pudding

There is only one thing in the world worse than being talked about, and that is not being talked about.

– Oscar Wilde

The one thing that customers have always rated highest in the sales world is trust, which is a direct reflection on the integrity of the individual. The primary reason people will choose not to buy from you is lack of trust.

– Zig Ziglar

I would like to say it was a restful night, but I would be lying if I did. I tossed and turned all night, thinking about what Phoebus said in the car. Luckily I could sleep in a bit, as Viator had some business to attend to that morning. I got to The Office Space around ten o'clock, and Viator was already there chatting with some of the others there.

"Good morning," he said, leading me into the conference room and looking at me a little closer. "You look tired. What's going on?"

I don't know how the man did it, but he had a knack for looking at you and knowing what question you were going to ask or that you were wrestling with a decision.

I said, "To be honest, I didn't sleep well last night. After I left you, on the way back to the hotel, Phoebus came across the screen in the car and…"

Viator interrupted me. "He did what? Tell me exactly what happened."

I relayed the story to him as he sat intently listening.

He shook his head and said, "I knew that would happen, but I didn't think they would be that brazen and bold. They are working overtime for sure."

At this point, I wasn't sure who to believe. Doubt gnawed at the corners of my mind, whispering words of caution and uncertainty. But then I was reminded of the old saying, "You have to break some eggs to make an omelet." I know I had lost clients in the past for various reasons its just part of doing businesses. Something in my gut told me to keep pushing, that I was doing the right thing sticking it out with Viator.

I looked at Viator and said, "What's on the agenda for today?"

"I'm glad you asked. Yesterday we covered the landing pages, and there was a section on testimonials. I wanted to focus on what I call the 'Social Proof' aspect of what you need to do."

"I know you mentioned it, but will you elaborate on it, please?"

Viator reached into his bag, pulled out two books, and flipped through the pages of the first one until he found the page he was looking for.

"John Jantsch, the author of *The Referral Engine*, says, 'Human beings are physiologically wired to make referrals. That's why so many businesses can grow and thrive by tapping this business-building strategy alone.'[1] So when it comes to marketing your business on the web, you need to take some of the same things you would do offline to the online space. For example, back in the day (and somewhat today), word-of-mouth is huge—especially for those who live in a rural area, like us. But as the younger generations become your buyers, they will rely more and more on the web to find the social proof they need to feel comfortable before reaching out or hiring you.

"Dr. Cialdini says this in his book, *Influence: The Psychology of Persuasion*:

> The principle [of social proof] states that we determine what is correct by finding out what other people think is correct. Importantly, the principle applies to the way we decide what constitutes correct behavior. We view an action as correct in a given situation to the degree that we see others performing it. As a result, advertisers love to inform us when a product is the "fastest growing" or "largest selling" because they don't have to convince us directly that their product is good; they need only show that many others think so, which often seems proof enough. [2]

"You see, when people don't know what they want or if something is good, we look to others for the answer. This is why referrals, word-of-mouth, testimonials, and social proof are so vital to any business. Take, for example, the humble shopping cart."

"A shopping cart," I said, questioning what it had to do with all this.

"Yes. The shopping cart we have today has its roots in social proof."

"No way," I protested. "You've got to explain that one to me."

"Back in 1934, Sylvan Goldman owned a small chain of grocery stores. At the time, there were only baskets for people to use to purchase groceries, and the customers would stop shopping when the baskets were full or too heavy. He developed a contraption that had two large metal baskets and wheels. However, his customers didn't take to it at first. After trying everything he could to promote their use, he finally hired people to come in and use them. Then his true customers began using them.[3] Do you understand why?"

"Social proof, I assume?"

"Yes. Because people saw others use the carts, they started doing it themselves, and it just compounds from there.

"Another example of social proof is the canned laugh or applause tracks found in Hollywood TV shows. Experiments have shown that using these tracks leads to more laughs and people thinking the show is funnier, unfortunately, than it actually is.[4] This raises the question: What is the best type of social proof?"

Grabbing a marker from the table, Viator stood and wrote the three types of social proof on the whiteboard:

- Word-of-mouth and Referrals
- Testimonials
- Reviews
- Referrals

"Let's talk specifically about referrals.

- Word-of-mouth and Referrals
- Testimonials
- Reviews

"Referrals come down to trust. We have all heard the saying that bad news travels fast. And you and I both know that in a rural area, *all* news travels fast. Given the limited population in a rural area, if you aren't trustworthy, you won't be in business for long.

"John Jantsch echoes this, saying, 'Trust is the most important reason a recommendation is made and, conversely, lack of trust is the single greatest reason referrals don't happen.'[5] In other words, if you want to be referred to, people have to know, like, and trust you!"

TESTIMONIALS

"Like referrals, testimonials help show the social proof that people crave and help people see others like them. Just like we talked about the NASCAR area on the pages of your website, a testimonial shows your prospects that you have worked with others like them."

"I see what you are saying, but how important are they? I mean, will they help that much?" I inquired, seeking a clearer understanding.

"The short answer is that testimonials are extremely valuable in the social proof aspect. Testimonials show that people, like your prospects, like your services enough to tell others about them. A good testimonial will explain why a client came to you in the first place, that your services helped them, and how their life is better. They are also great for SEO, as they can also show up in the SERPs."

"How so?" I asked.

"The search engines index everything on the page, so if there is a keyword or keyword phrase that shows up on your page and in your testimonials, they may use that page on the SERPs. This is especially true if they are searching for you and a specific keyword or phrase."

"What if I don't have any or have trouble getting them?"

"That is a two-part question, so let's address the trouble getting them first. Sometimes you have to hold a client's hand to get a good testimonial. Sometimes you have to almost write it for them, like a fill-in-the-blank-type offering. However, you have to be really careful if you do it that way. You don't want all your testimonials to be the same. And as long as you don't fake them, you'll be fine. You don't want to lose people's trust by faking your testimonials.

"Now for the second part of that question: the lack of testimonials. If you are new to the business or in an industry where people might not want to give testimonials for various reasons due to embarrassment or privacy, you can use statistics."

"But didn't Mark Twain say, 'There are three kinds of lies: Lies, [expletive] Lies, and Statistics'?"

"Yes, but the good news is that there are solid sources of statistics on anything and everything; you will just have to dig into the sources and make a judgment call. If you question the validity of the source, then don't use it. But if you do find a good one, use it to your advantage! But when it comes to statistics and numbers you generally need to make them simple for people to understand."

Viator went over to the shelf by the wall and ran his fingers along the spines of the books on the shelf, then stopped and pulled one out. He flipped through the pages. Setting it in front of me, and he said, "Take a look at this."

The book was *Making Numbers Count* by Chip Heath and Karla Starr. He pointed to a passage that was already highlighted. It read:

More often than not, we don't even make sense of the complicated number in the first place. Alfred Taubman, former CEO of the A&W restaurant chain and author of Threshold Resistance, learned that lesson the hard way when his company tried to introduce a third-pound burger at the same price as the McDonald's quarter-pounder. More than half the customers thought they were being ripped off. "Why should we pay the same amount for less meat?" they said.

The value of the new A&W burger depended on consumers comparing two fractions: 1/3 and 1/4. But fractions are difficult for everyone because they're parts of things as opposed to whole objects. We like to count things, and fractions don't equal "things." So, we jump to the closest available whole numbers. four is bigger than three, so we mistakenly infer that a 1/4-pounder is a bigger burger than a 1/3-pounder..[6]

Viator went on to explain that the authors also highlight three rules for numbers, which are:

- **Simpler Is Better**: Round with enthusiasm.[7]
- **Concrete Is Better**: Use whole numbers to describe whole objects, not decimals, fractions, or percentages.[8]
- **Follow the Rules but Defer to Expertise**: Rules 1 and 2 may be trumped by expert knowledge.[9]

REVIEWS

"Next on the list are reviews. They are very much like testimonials, but these don't live on your website natively. They are usually found around the web on directories and review sites."

"I have seen those when I look for things," I said, "but I have heard that people don't read them, or they are often faked."

Viator said, "They most certainly do matter, so much so that in 2017 Google placed more value on them, especially as it related to local results."

"Yes, there are 'businesses'—" He made air quotes with his hands. "—that will generate fake reviews, both good and bad. But people have learned to spot them whether they realize it or not."

Some things to look out for include the following:[10, 11]

- Names that don't match the region or population
- Star ratings only with no text
- Low star ratings with no text
- Short, vague, and quickly written
- Excessive enthusiasm
- The reviewer has left very few or left several reviews in a short time span
- Lacks detail or lacks a true experience with your service
- Includes first-person pronouns
- Has more verbs than nouns

"Now, let me go back and address the question about how much people use them. I mentioned that Google includes it as part of their algorithm. As Todd Caponi said in *The Transparency Sale*, 'consumers trust reviews and act upon what they learn from reviews. Good online reviews drive traffic to your website and ultimately to the front door of your business.'[12]

"He also says that:

> Today, children (aka "our future buyers") are growing up surrounded by reviews and feedback on everything they interact with. Adults are becoming dependent on them as well. These present and future buyers have an expectation of transparency, where their decisions are influenced by user-submitted feedback listed right alongside the options they are deciding upon. In some cases, we have even become incapable of making a selection without the aid of these reviews.[13]

WORDS OF CAUTION AROUND ALL THESE

Viator said, "I have to make sure you pay attention to all review sites and directories that your clients will typically use." He rattled off a few of the top ones. "Now, these sites will come and go, and new ones will pop up all the time. Just try to keep a watchful eye out.

"Social media is another place where you will want to try to get reviews, but you also need to watch out here, as one bad review can travel fast. The next thing you know, you could have gone viral for something you had no clue about—or worse, no control over."

RESPOND TO REVIEWS

"You always need to respond to reviews, both good and bad."

"Both?" I asked.

"Yep. I know it's more work, but you need to respond as best you can to all of them. If you come across a negative one, then respond and, if needed, take it offline. Don't be vindictive about it and try to go Tony Soprano on someone. I once spoke with a prospect that gave off that vibe. Looking back, I'm glad I never worked with them."

ASKING FOR REVIEWS, TESTIMONIALS, AND REFERRALS

"There are lots of ways to get referrals, but you have to first believe that you deserve them, so I ask you: Do you believe your business is referable?"

I nodded in agreement.

"Now, do you know the best time to ask for a referral?"

"I guess when I'm finished with the job?"

"Possibly. It depends on the circumstances. It might be that it is a perfect time, it might be three, five, or seven days later, or it could be as many as six to nine months. What matters is that you ask when you know they are happy with what you did. You also must ensure they understand why they are important and how to leave one. You may even want to help coach them about what you think would be good to mention in the review, but you shouldn't go as far as writing it for them."

INCENTIVES FOR REVIEWS

My curiosity was piqued, I couldn't help but inquire further. "Can I offer a discount or a gift card for someone to leave a review?"

"No!" he said emphatically, his tone leaving no room for doubt.

Surprised by his unwavering stance, "Really?" I asked.

"Yep. You see, it can be seen as an attempt to manipulate or influence the content of the review. Not to mention, the big players all have strict policies against it in their terms of services, and they can even penalize you for it.

"The bottom line, is you need to remember that reviews are meant to reflect people's honest and unbiased opinions, and any attempt to influence or manipulate the opinions would undermine their credibility."

CAN SOCIAL PROOF BOOST SEO?

Viator explained that social proof could help a rural small business's SEO.

He said, "All the search engines consider social proof as a factor when determining the relevance and authority of a website. When a business has a high volume of recent positive reviews or a website has backlinks from reputable sources with a high authority score, the search engines see this as a signal that this business or website can be a trusted and valuable resource for its users.

"Another way to think about it is if you ask a friend for a recommendation, they refer you to someone, and then when you talk to them, you realize how knowledgeable they are about the subject."

"That makes a lot of sense," I said.

Viator continued, his tone contemplative. "Now think about this: Negative reviews can be just as powerful as positive ones," he asserted, prompting my curiosity further.

"How so?" I asked.

"Well, it goes back to our primal ancestors and our basic survival instincts. We, as humans, are social creatures, and we have survived because of our cooperation and communication. When we encounter danger, our brain's natural response is to go into a heightened state of awareness. In other words, our lizard brain takes over, triggering our 'fight or flight' response."

He went on to explain, "We want to warn others about the danger as a way to protect not only ourselves, but also those we care about, including our family and friends.

"You see, the act of warning others helps us to validate what we have been through. It helps us to process and cope with the experience by sharing it with others and receiving their support and understanding. The bottom line is that warning others isn't just about keeping them safe; it's also about helping ourselves feel better too.

"An example would be when my son was diagnosed with Type 1 Diabetes. We went to the hospital for what we thought was going to be an ulcer or appendicitis. But within seconds, our life changed when they tested his blood sugar, and it was literally off the chart of the meter.

"Sitting in the emergency room, I searched the internet and social media to help understand the disease. And now, I use social media to better understand what he is going through. I also share the symptoms in person and online before diagnosis so fellow parents can be prepared."

"Wow, I never thought about it like that," I said.

HOW TO USE SOCIAL PROOF

Viator asked me if I could think of ways I could use social proof with my business. I thought for a moment and rattled off a couple of possible examples.

He then said, "According to Daniel Eisenberg in a 2002 Time Magazine article he wrote, 'Some marketers have found they don't need people at all to spread the word. Even before the trendy energy drink Red Bull hit the shelves in England a few years ago, a London agency called Cake Creative Consultancy filled sidewalk trash cans and pub tables in Newcastle with empty cans of the stuff. Cake executives readily talk about the campaign, but in a sign of how sensitive stealth marketing has become.'[14]

"Another example might be the 'exclusive club' with a line around the building. Because there is a line, people may think the club is bigger or more exclusive than it really is. Other examples included saying simple things like 'this is our most popular service' or 'these are selling faster than we can keep them in stock.'

"Whenever you utilize social proof, you need to make sure to show how similar the person or the situation is to the one you're sharing it with. Does all that make sense?"

"Yeah, it does, actually."

"Great." Viator grinned and pulled his phone from his pocket. "I will call us a pizza, and we can keep working if that is ok with you."

"Sounds great," I said.

"Perfect. I know just who to call!"

"Ghostbusters?"

He laughed. "Not quite, but I admire your thinking."

10 | Everything SEO

Marketing on the web is not about generic banner ads designed to trick people with neon color or wacky movement. It is about understanding the keywords and phrases that our buyers are using, and creating the content that they seek.

– David Meerman Scott

[the Internet is] a giant machine designed to give people what they want.

– Evan Williams

While we waited for our food to arrive, Viator seized the opportunity to dig into the world of search engine optimization (SEO) and its various components. He turned his attention towards me and posed a question. "Do you understand what search engine optimization is?"

I responded honestly. "I think I do. I have heard people talk about it, and I have people tell me my 'SEO' is bad, but that is about the extent of my knowledge," I said.

"Okay, that helps me know where to start.

"When it comes to search engines, there are three big players—Google, Bing, and Yahoo—in the United States. According to Statcounter, in May of 2023, Google had 89.1% of the market share. Bing and Yahoo had 8.6% combined, and I combined them because Bing powers Yahoo search. The bottom line is that nearly nine out of ten people will use Google, and the other one in ten will use Bing or Yahoo.

"When it comes to search engines, they all behave similarly and follow a similar process to find content. Those can be broken down into crawling, indexing, and ranking.

"During the first step in the process, the search engine crawls your website. In other words, the search engines have software that goes across the web, looking for and collecting information from web pages. You may hear them called web crawlers, bots, or spiders. These bots follow links from one web page to the next, collecting information on the content, keywords, images, and links on each page they visit.

"Now, you would think that just because a site has been crawled, it would show up on the search results pages (SERPs), but it's handed off to the indexing process. The servers then process, organize, and store all the information collected in an index.

"The last step is to take and rank the information in the index and display it on the SERPs. This is where things get really complicated because there isn't one person who fully knows what goes into the algorithm. What we know is that it considers the content quality, relevance, authority, and user engagement."

I looked at him and said, "Just so I'm clear, my website has to get crawled, indexed, and then it can rank?"

"Yep, that's basically it. So our goal is to do everything we can to make it easier for the search engines to find and crawl your content, index it, and then rank it."

"I had no idea that all that was going on behind the scenes when I did a search," I said.

Viator glanced toward the glass doors of The Office Space and exclaimed, "Ah, the pizza is here! Mind coming to help me?"

We walked to the door and parked out front was an old ice cream truck, complete with the cone on top. But the body of the truck was definitely pizza-inspired. The side of the truck read, "Slice, Slice, Baby: A place to Stop, Collaborate, and Eat."

As we approached the truck, the tantalizing aroma of cooking pizza wafted through the air. Stepping up to the truck's window, we were greeted by friendly and energetic faces.

They greeted Viator by name as they handed him the steaming pizza box. I couldn't help but notice the attention to detail as the box itself boasted a hand-drawn image of the truck and a quote that read, "A slice a day keeps the hunger at bay."

As we walked back in and set the pizza box on the conference room table, I asked Viator if all the restaurants here were named after puns.

He looked at me and said, "Not all of them. Just the best ones."

I just shook my head, opened the box, and picked up a slice.

As we ate, Viator explained that SEO was really about optimizing the content on a website—in this case, mine—for the search engines. Between bites of pizza, he told me about the three main ways to optimize a site: Technical SEO, On-Page, and Off-Page.

TECHNICAL SEO

"Technical SEO involves optimizing a website's technical side, backend, or code to improve its ranking and visibility on the SERPs. In other words, it covers everything related to the underlying structure of your website, and it helps your site meet the requirements the search engines need to easily crawl your site and ultimately find their way through your content."

Viator wiped his hands on a napkin and went up to the whiteboard, and wrote the following list:

1. Site Speed

2. Responsive Design

3. Robots.txt

4. XML Sitemap

5. SSL Certificate

6. Structured Data

7. Canonical Tags

8. 404 Pages

9. URL Structure

10. Image Optimization

11. Broken Links

12. Crawl Errors

13. Hreflang Tags

14. Pagination

15. Redirects

1. Site Speed
2. Responsive Design or Mobile-friendly Design
3. Robots.txt
4. XML Sitemap
5. SSL Certificate
6. Structured Data
7. Canonical Tags
8. 404 pages
9. URL Structure
10. Image Optimization
11. Broken Links
12. Crawl Errors
13. Hreflang Tags
14. Pagination
15. Redirects

He stepped back and took another bite of his pizza, looking over the list.

I looked at it and said, "I don't know how to pronounce some of those words, let alone what they are."

"Don't worry; you shouldn't need to know what all of those are unless you plan to DIY your site. But there are a couple there that I need to ensure you are aware of.

"The first is site speed. How fast your site loads is critical, especially if you are in a rural area. There might be good broadband in one part of your area, but there could be a broadband wasteland just a few hundred feet away. Those people might rely on other means to access the Internet, such as cell phones. Therefore, you have to make sure your site loads quickly for them.

"Next is responsive design—also called mobile-friendly design—and having an SSL certificate. Now, I know we already talked about both, but it bears repeating that these are a big factor these days."

1. Title Tags

2. Meta Descriptions

3. Header Tags

4. Keyword(s)
   and Keyword Phrases

5. Image optimization

6. Alt Text

7. Content Optimization

ON-PAGE SEO

"On-page SEO is the process of optimizing the content, meta tags, headlines, images, and internal linking on your web pages and your website. There are two main goals for On-page SEO:

1. Improve the competitiveness of the individual web pages on the SERPs to attract more relevant organic traffic.
2. Align your website's overall content with the intent of both users and Google indexers.

"Now that we know what our goal is with on-page SEO, let's break down parts," Viator said, turning to write the following on the board:

1. Title Tags
2. Meta Descriptions
3. Header Tags
4. Keyword(s) and Keyword Phrases
5. Image Optimization
6. Alt Text
7. Content Optimization

He looked over the list and said, "I think these will be the last things we talk about, at least for today."

He then went on to explain each in more detail.

1. TITLE TAGS

Picture this: you are reading a chapter book, and each chapter has a title. The title usually gives you some clue as to what the chapter is about. A title tag is similar, but instead of a chapter, it's a page, article, or blog on your website.

And just like the title helps you understand what the page is about, it also helps the search engines too. The title tag helps everyone by providing a concise and accurate description of your content.

Another notable feature is that the title will show up on the SERPs, at the top of the browser tabs, and when a page is shared on social media.

2. META DESCRIPTIONS

Meta descriptions are what shows up underneath the title tag on the SERPs. These are around 160 characters or less and explains to the searcher what your page is about. They should entice searchers to click on your link and visit your page.

3. HEADER TAGS

A header tag is like a label that helps organize a webpage or blog post. The most important header tag is usually H1, which is like the title of a chapter in a book. You should start with one H1, as this tells the reader and the search engines what your page is about in about 60-80 characters.

Then as you move down the page, you may have an H2, H3, etc. to help you organize your content. You might want to think about them as subtitles or subheadings that divide the content into smaller pieces.

Essentially, you want to make the web page easier to read and understand for people and search engines alike.

4. KEYWORD(S) AND KEYWORD PHRASES

Keywords and keyword phrases are the terms that users enter into search engines to find what they are looking for.

For example, you might want to bake chocolate chip cookies, so you search for "chocolate chip cookies." But you might need something more specific, like "low-carb chocolate chip cookies" or "keto chocolate chip cookies."

Now, you might still need to refine it more, so you search for "what is the best low-carb chocolate chip cookie recipe for diabetics."

The difference between short-tail and long-tail keywords is the difference between using just one or two words versus a whole sentence or phrase. The first examples represent short-tail keywords since they are shorter, whereas the last example represents long-tail keywords.

5. IMAGE OPTIMIZATION

If you recall, I have spoken a lot about making the pages load quickly. Images are one of the biggest culprits of poor page load time. There is a balance between the "weight" of the image and the "quality." This means you sometimes must decide to sacrifice a little bit of image quality to make the download size smaller.

6. ALT TEXT

Alt Text is an abbreviation for Alternative Text and was initially developed to help describe images. Alt text plays a significant role in website accessibility. If we sprinkle some keywords into the image description, we can use alt text to help with SEO.

7. CONTENT OPTIMIZATION

I feel like I have drilled the need for good quality content into you thus far, so I will just say this: Make sure you write content that answers people's questions.

OFF-PAGE SEO

"Now, when it comes to off-page SEO, it's a bit of a black box because you will do things, but it's harder to see the true return on most of it."

The look on my face must have spelled pure confusion because he said, "Let me explain.

"You see, off-page SEO is everything you do off your website to make it rank better. This will include things like:

- Link Building
- Social Media Marketing
- Guest Posting
- Brand Mentions

"Off-page SEO helps the search engines determine a website's popularity, authority, and trustworthiness and goes back to the E-E-A-T. You see, by increasing your E-E-A-T, people will naturally want to start linking back to you, and thus you start getting high-quality backlinks.

WHAT ARE BACKLINKS?

My curiosity piqued, "You have said the word backlink; what is a backlink?" I asked.

"Ah. A backlink is simply a link from one site to another—or in your case, a link from someone else's site to yours.

"Another way to think about it is to imagine a piece of research written by a scholar. The scholar will have referenced others' work in their article. Then they hope another scholar will pick up *their* research and reference it. Have this happen enough, and the researchers' authority will go through the roof! Now replace the scholar with your website. If you have a blog or a page on your site, your goal is to get others to link to it, thus sending your website and your authority through the roof!

"But keep this in mind: not all links are created equal. High-quality backlinks from reputable websites are more valuable than low-quality backlinks from spammy or irrelevant websites. Therefore, you need to focus on building high-quality backlinks from relevant and authoritative sources to improve your website's ranking and visibility.

"Do you have a better understanding of it all now?"

"Yeah, I think I do."

BLACK HAT SEO: WHAT NOT TO DO

"Okay, let's talk about things you shouldn't do—also known as 'black hat techniques'—from an SEO standpoint," he said.

KEYWORD STUFFING

Keyword stuffing is a technique in which the page owner will attempt to cram a page with the same keyword (or slight variations of it) over and over again.

Here is an example with the keyword "Deep Sea Fishing."

> Deep sea fishing is an exciting fishing adventure for those who love fishing in the deep blue sea. With deep sea fishing trips, you'll experience the thrill of catching large deep sea fish while enjoying the beauty of the ocean. If you're interested in deep sea fishing, make sure to book a deep sea fishing charter and learn all about deep sea fishing techniques. Whether you're a beginner or an experienced deep sea fishing enthusiast, deep sea fishing is an unforgettable experience that will make you fall in love with

deep sea fishing all over again. Don't forget to bring your deep sea fishing gear and prepare for the deep sea fishing trip of a lifetime!

Obviously, that isn't providing any value to the searcher, and frankly, it's hard to read.

HIDDEN TEXT

Some website owners or marketers will try to hide text by using the same color as the background or using tiny fonts. This was an older trick that was used to stuff extra keywords without making the page look cluttered. Search engines nowadays can detect hidden text and will often penalize sites that use it.

CLOAKING

Cloaking involves showing different content to search engines and users. For example, a site might display helpful information to users, but search engines see a page filled with keywords.

DUPLICATE CONTENT OR PLAGIARISM

I have seen places where an "author" will copy the text directly from one site, paste it into another, and call it their own. While this was much more prevalent in the past, you will still see it on some of the social media sites that allow you to post longer-form content.

Now, this isn't to say you can't quote something you or others have said before. You just need to make sure you link back to the source so the search engines knows where it came from.

He looked at me and said, "What do you think? Are things starting to become clearer?"

"Yeah," I nodded in agreement and said. "I mean, there is a lot to keep up with, and I don't know how you know all this stuff."

He laughed. "Well, I have several years of experience, but to be honest, I read a lot of books by people smarter than me. I also read a lot of email newsletters which help me keep up with everything, and I listen to lots of podcasts."

"Well, it shows," I said.

Viator looked at the time and said, "You want to call it a day?"

"Yeah, I won't lie. I'm tired. It might be best."

"Let's pack it up and hit it up first thing in the morning, then. Meet you the 9-to-5 Grind at eight o'clock?"

"Sounds great! See you then!"

11 | Welcome to Social Media

Social media is not about the exploitation of technology, but service to community.

— Simon Mainwaring

Back at my hotel, I lay in bed and closed my eyes. My mind wandered over what Viator had said that day, which was becoming a nightly occurrence. I also thought about my business and wondered what was happening while I was still stuck here.

I recalled all the time and effort I had put into my business—the late nights and early mornings, and all the risks I had taken. And yet, despite all that, it seemed as though my efforts were not going to pay off. And to be honest, this was the same, constant feeling of despair that always seemed to hit me at night.

Who knew why it always hit me at night? Maybe it was because the days were packed with work, errands, and a million little tasks. But despite the rush and the hustle of running a business.

But at the same time, after working with Viator, I felt a sense of satisfaction and contentment.

I woke up the next morning feeling refreshed and ready for whatever Viator had to talk about. As I was getting ready, I heard a tap on my door. Thinking it might have been Viator, I walked over and checked the peephole—but there wasn't anyone there. It might've been a kid knocking on random doors, just being a kid.

As I turned, I heard the sound of crumpling paper under my foot. I looked down and saw an envelope. Inside was a note that said, "Meet us at 'Livin' on Biscuits, Gravy, and a Prayer' at 7:00 AM," and a map of how to get there. It was signed by "The Trio."

I felt a chill run down my spine and wondered if I should go, but I thought, what do I have to lose at this point? It could be a free meal and better than the continental breakfast of instant eggs and waffles. I hurried and got ready. As I was about to walk out the door, I shot Viator a message soliciting his thoughts if I should go. I waited ten minutes but never heard from him, so I decided to go.

As I got to the Livin' on Biscuits, Gravy, and a Prayer, I saw Phoebus and Otto standing outside waiting for me.

"Hello again," Phoebus said with a sly smile.

Otto said, "Come on in; Constanze has a table waiting for us."

As we walked to the table, Constanze stood up and said, "Hello again," with a smile almost robotic.

As I sat down and looked over the menu, Constanze told me what was good. Pleased by her helpful demeanor, I figured this might not be as bad as I thought it would be.

Our waiter, who introduced himself as Jack, came and took our order. The tiro attempted to make some small talk while we waited on the food to arrive. Thankfully it didn't take long, and when it did get to the table, Constanze went straight to the point, "Let's get down to why we asked you here: it's to talk to you about Viator."

"Yes," said Phoebus. "Viator won't be able to help you like he says he can."

"What do you mean?" I asked, trying to keep my voice steady.

"Viator is a false hope," Phoebus replied, his eyes gleaming. "He is telling you what you need to do, but in reality, it's a hard road, and it could only make things worse."

Otto nodded sternly. "Right. His ideas are too radical, his methods too unconventional. If you follow him, you'll only end up causing yourself more trouble. You would be much better to double down on what you have been doing than to follow his advice."

I shook my head, trying to ignore the voice of doubt that was starting to creep into my mind. "I don't believe you," I said firmly.

But Phoebus only laughed. "You're so naive," he said. "Viator always says he can help, but this time is different. The challenges you face now are too great."

"I don't follow you," I said.

Constanze and Otto only shook their heads. "The world is a complicated place, and change is not always for the better," Constanze said. "If you keep listening to him, you'll only end up regretting it."

I frowned, feeling a sense of frustration building inside of me. "I don't understand why you always try to discourage me," I said.

Otto said, "We are just trying to protect you, and what you know has worked in the past."

"We just have a harder time seeing how what Viator does works," Constanze said.

I felt a wave of anger wash over me, and I had to fight to keep from lashing out at them. I said, "You make some valid points, but honestly, I want to at least see what else he has to say."

With that, the rest of the meal was tense but cordial.

As we finished, I thanked them and headed to The Office Space to meet Viator.

When I got to The Office Space, it was about ten minutes after eight o'clock. Viator looked at me and jokingly said, "Did you get lost?"

"No," I said. "Otto, Constanze, and Phoebus took me to breakfast at Livin' on Biscuits, Gravy, and a Prayer."

"Really?"

"Yep. The food was good, but I must say the conversation wasn't." I laughed wryly and proceeded to tell him what had happened.

Viator then asked me, "What do you think? It sounds like you trust what I'm telling you—but what does your gut tell you."

"My jury is still out, but I feel like I'm getting closer to making a decision."

"Fair enough," he said.

Viator paused, looked deep in thought, then said, "I tell you what. Let's take a ride this morning. I have something I want to show you."

Viator called a car, and we headed out from The Office Space. We headed down a major road, and it was scenic and beautiful. But then things started to change. It began to get murky, with signs everywhere. It felt almost like the tourist towns where every business thinks they can put up a bigger sign and get people in the door. I couldn't help but think about the old song lyrics, "Sign, sign. Everywhere a sign. Blockin' out the scenery. Breakin' my mind."

What was interesting about all the signs was they looked a lot like social media posts. I saw pictures of kids and lots of people with duck lips and peace signs. And like when I got here, things looked like digital screens, I saw people like and comment on posts. I saw people getting into what could be considered shouting matches over text, over trivial things. I saw videos of people dancing and people doing stupid things. In my mind, I knew that this was what social media had turned into, and it was one reason I had only done the minimum with the business.

Viator must have read my mind. He looked at me and said, "I guess by now you have figured out where we are."

I looked around and asked, "Are we in Facebook?"

"Close," he said. "We are really in the social media section of town."

We went up the road just a little, and Viator then pointed out a massive wall that looked as if it was designed to keep a seven nation army out. "Over there, behind that wall with all the signs sticking up above it, is Facebook. And as Bob said, it is a walled garden, for obvious reasons."

He continued pointing out all the different areas and explained that social media is a blessing and a curse. "You see all the social media starlets with the bigger signs? They like to think they have a thriving business. But what happens when the road gets moved, or the ground beneath them vanishes?"

"PIVOT," I said in my best Ross Geller impression.

"Not exactly, but I like where your mind is headed," he said with a smile. "What really happens is they stand to lose it all if they haven't found other ways to engage with their audience. So, in essence, they do have to PIVOT or be prepared to. The bottom line is: you don't build your business on rented land."

"That is pretty profound," I said.

"Well, I would like to take credit for it, but I actually heard it first from Joe Pulizzi, who contributed it to John Battelle.

"Battelle wrote:

If you're going to build something, don't build on land someone else already owns. You want your own land, your own domain, your own sovereignty.[1]

"Facebook opened to the public on September 26, 2006, and by late 2007, it had over 100,000 businesses on the platform.[2] Now flash forward to the 2010s, and Facebook was a powerhouse, and businesses wanted to be there because consumers were there.

"Author, speaker and thought leader, Robert Rose explains that 'Battelle was referencing the growing notion among brands at the time that websites and other owned media were unneeded.'[3]

"Now think about this: computer security expert Bruce Schneier said, 'Don't make the mistake of thinking you're Facebook's customer, you're not—you're the product. Its customers are the advertisers.[4] But the same goes for all the social media platforms. You, the user, are the product. Social media will always exist to make money, and the only way to do that is to either charge you, sell ads, or both!"

He went on to say, "This isn't a new concept. According to the Quote Investigator, 'In 1973 the artists Richard Serra and Carlota Fay Schoolman broadcast a short video titled 'Television Delivers People'.[5]

"The video says: [6]

> Commercial television delivers 20 million people a minute.
>
> In commercial broadcasting, the viewer pays for the privilege of having himself sold.
>
> It is the consumer who is consumed.
>
> You are the product of T.V.
>
> You are delivered to the advertiser who is the customer.
>
> He consumes you.
>
> The viewer is not responsible for programming—
>
> You are the end product.

I rubbed the back of my neck with my hand. "You know, I have never really thought about it, but you bring up some good points."

"Now, I don't want you to think I'm completely against social media—because I'm not. Social media is good for generating awareness and is a way to promote your content freely, but you really need to have a strategy behind it and a way to take the audience with you or, at the least, to drive them to your own properties. In other words, don't abandon traditional marketing and advertising tactics in favor of social media or any other method until you know they work."

Viator continued, saying that, "If you want to use social media, do so with an open mind. Use it to build your business's reputation, be conversational, and keep the 'social' in social media."

THE GOOD, THE BAD, AND THE UGLY

The car pulled up and stopped in front of another coffee shop, The Social Cup. As we exited, I wondered how Viator drank so much coffee and still slept at night. We walked in, ordered a couple drinks, and took our seats at a nearby table.

"Since we are in the social district, I thought we could have a good discussion about the good, the bad, and the ugly sides of social media," Viator said. "Let's look at the good parts of social media first. How would you describe it?"

I went on to describe what I thought it was.

"That's not a bad definition; David Meerman Scott describes it as:

> …the way people share ideas, content, thoughts, and relationships online. Social media differs from so-called mainstream media in that anyone can create, comment on, and add to social media content. Social media can take the form of text, audio, video, images, and communities.
>
> The best way to think about social media is not in terms of the different technologies and tools but, rather, how those technologies and tools allow you to communicate directly with your buyers in places where they are congregating right now.[7]

Viator said, "Here is how I describe it.

"Social media is like the digital gathering place where everyone comes together to share the latest gossip, show off their perfect biscuit recipes, and post selfies with their pets. It can be a wonderful and almost magical place where you can keep up with your friends, family, and celebrities.

"However, as magical as it is, it can also be a huge time suck and a way to hide behind the facade of the perfect life or to procrastinate on real-life responsibilities. Think about how often you have heard someone say, 'I got sucked into watching videos till two o'clock in the morning,' or you hear about the couple that broke up or got a divorce, and someone says, 'They looked so happy on social media.'

"When I was in college, the way we communicated was with AOL Instant Messenger or AIM. You would be sitting at your desk, and someone would message you, and you would have a conversation. You used your 'away message' to convey your mood or tell your friends where you would be.

"Then Facebook came along, and college kids flocked to it for two reasons: because you had to have a college email address and because their parents weren't on it. They were free to talk about what they were really doing.

"I dabbled in Facebook, but I never took to it like my younger friends did. I graduated from grad school and started teaching. This was also about the same time that MySpace was popular, and I was encouraged to get an account 'so I could connect with students and promote the program,' which I did, and I let my Facebook account go dormant.

"Eventually, MySpace evolved and changed, and it's to the point now that some members of Generation Z (those born after 1997) have never even heard of it. From what I can tell now, it's more of a place to find music than to connect with people."

"What is hot today may not be hot tomorrow.

"I can remember having a conversation with the public information officer at the college after I transitioned to the marketing department, and she believed that social media (Facebook in general) would just be a fad. Little did she or I—or any of us for that matter—realize how integrated into our everyday lives it would become.

"All of this brings me to some of the good parts of social media:

1. As I mentioned before, social media allows us to stay connected with people. You are never more than a few taps away from knowing what your cousin's wife is making for dinner!
2. You can get 'news' faster, and I loosely use the term 'news.'
3. You can use it for shameless self-promotion. Social media can be your digital megaphone to tell the world about your small business.
4. You can use it for inspiration.
5. When you're feeling down or facing a difficult challenge, it can be a goldmine of support from people who've been there, done that, and got the t-shirt.

"With all the good social media brings, there is a downside. Dr. Robert Cialdini writes in *Influence: The Psychology of Persuasion, New and Expanded*, that:

> In 1713, Jonathan Swift declared in a famous line of poetry, "Tis an old maxim in the schools / That flattery's the food of fools." But he failed to tell us how eager people are to swallow those empty calories. For instance, with a remark as instructive as it is humorous, the comedic actor McLean Stevenson once described how his wife "tricked" him into marriage: "She said she liked me." Today, the "likes" frequently occur online and with a comparable effect on positive feelings. In a brain-imaging study, researchers found that when teenagers' social-media photos received lots of "likes," the reward sectors of their brains lit up like Christmas trees—the same reward sectors normally activated by such desirable events as eating chocolate or winning money.[8]

"He goes on to say that:

> Often, we don't realize our attitude toward something has been influenced by the number of times we have been exposed to it.
>
> In an age of "fake news," internet bots, and media-hogging politicians, it's alarming to think that people come to believe the communications they are exposed to most frequently, as it gives contemporary resonance to Nazi propaganda chief Joseph Goebels's assertion, "Repeat a lie often enough and it becomes the truth." Particularly unsettling are the related findings that even far-fetched claims—the kind of allegations favored by fake-news creators—become more believable with repetition.[9]

"The problem is that it gets worse, as Dr. Cialdini also references a story that happened in later 2019. Rumors were being spread on social media that men in sketchy white vans were abducting women for sex trafficking and selling their body parts. It got so bad that the mayor of Baltimore at the time, Bernard Young, warned young women to avoid them. The basis for the claim was 'It was all over Facebook.'[10, 11]

"That is one of the very reasons I use the word 'news' loosely when I talk about social media. It has become far too easy to spread information without the basis of facts."

As Viator paused and took the last sip from his cup, I said, "Tell me how you really feel about it."

Viator laughed. "I know it sounds like I hate it, but I don't. I hate what it has become. I have seen social media do wonders, and I have even gotten clients and had clients get clients through it. But the thing is that social media is just a tool and should be treated as such."

THE KEY TO SUCCESSFUL SOCIAL MEDIA

Back at The Office Space, we sat in our usual seats at the conference room table and started talking about the keys to a successful social media strategy.

Viator said, "Let's look at the strategy you need to employ to be effective. According to Gary Vaynerchuk:

> Social media requires that business leaders start thinking like small-town shop owners...
>
> This means taking the long view and avoiding short-term benchmarks to gauge progress... In short, business leaders are going to have to relearn the ethics and skills our great-grandparents' generation used in building their own businesses and took for granted... [O]nly the companies that can figure out how to mind their manners in a very old-fashioned way—and do it authentically—are going to have a prayer of competing.[12]
>
> Engagement has to be heartfelt or it won't work.
>
> You cannot underestimate people's ability to spot a soulless, bureaucratic tactic a million miles away. It's a big reason why so

many companies that have dipped a toe in social media waters have failed miserably.[13]

"In other words, when it comes to social media, we have to remember to keep the 'social' in social media. No matter what we do, if we lose sight of that, it's a waste."

He then went to the whiteboard and wrote out the following:

1. How and where do your clients use social media?
2. What is your competition doing, and where
3. What is your current marketing strategy, and how will social complement it?
4. What is the ultimate goal?
5. Can you be present and be social?

1. How and where do your clients use social media?
2. What is your competition doing and where?
3. What is your current marketing strategy, and how will social media complement it?
4. What is the ultimate goal?
5. Can you be present and be social?

Stepping back, he said, "let's look at the first item there."

1. HOW AND WHERE DO YOUR CLIENTS USE SOCIAL MEDIA?

The first thing you need to ask yourself is: is my target audience using *this* platform? Are they looking for my services on it as well? Do they want to connect and communicate with me here?

Joe Pulizzi says in *Content Inc.*, "If you are just getting serious about your social media distribution efforts, it's best to start small. Consider the top social platforms used in your industry niche, and see where the largest concentration of your target audience member is congregating."[14]

One of the biggest issues I see is people thinking they need to be on a platform because someone's father's brother's nephew's cousin's former roommate told them they needed to be there.

2. WHAT IS YOUR COMPETITION DOING AND WHERE?

Here is where you have to spy a bit and look at what your competitors are doing.

To quote Joe Pulizzi again:

Choose the channels where you can build and engage with a genuine community, and focus your attention on those. Study what others are doing in this space, so you can learn what people respond to the most favorably. By "others," I don't mean your competition, but rather anyone who may be taking your audience's attention away from your social media content (such as your influencer group). Ask yourself how you can be more useful or entertaining than other content providers.

While it makes sense to choose the primary channels you will focus on, the landscape is changing quickly, and it's important to experiment to keep your social media content offers fresh and current.

It doesn't make sense to start using a platform simply because it's become trendy or because your competitors have a presence there.[15]

In other words, are they on Meerkat, the Trestle Board, or Google Plus? If they are, that doesn't mean you need to be.

3. WHAT IS YOUR CURRENT MARKETING STRATEGY AND HOW WILL SOCIAL MEDIA COMPLEMENT IT?

When it comes to social media, you need to know where it fits in the big picture. If you aren't ready, it will become a beast that can't easily be tamed.

One big mistake I often see is that people will think social media is a cheap and easy way to reach people. Like Bob Hoffman says, "Many self-proclaimed social media 'gurus' would have you believe that social media is the future of all marketing and that if you're not dedicating most or all of your marketing resources to social media, you're a Luddite who'll soon be out of business."[16]

Joe Pulizzi also says:

> While I believe that any fan, follower, or subscriber can be a good thing, they are not equal in value.
>
> Over the past few years, Facebook has made drastic changes to its platform to hide posts from pages, including:
> - Posts that solely push to buy a product or install an app
> - Posts that push people to enter promotions and sweepstakes with no real context
> - Posts that reuse ad content exactly
> - Posts that direct people to an outside website
>
> This makes sense for Facebook's business model, but it also means that Facebook has the right not to show certain posts.
>
> Because of that algorithm, some businesses have seen organic reach (traffic that you don't pay for) on Facebook fall to 1 percent or less. At the same time, Scott Linabarger, former content marketing director at Cleveland Clinic, says that some posts still perform well organically on Facebook. It really doesn't matter. You should leverage Facebook however you can, but you need to know that Facebook controls the ultimate reach, not you.[17]

4. WHAT IS THE ULTIMATE GOAL?

When it comes to social media, you can't dive in headfirst. You must have a goal in mind. Social media can and will become a major time-suck and take over your life if you don't. Personally, I like to use social media to further a conversation and drive traffic back to your website, where there is a message that you can control.

5. CAN YOU BE PRESENT AND BE SOCIAL?

While social media can be automated, you still need to be prepared to answer questions. Again, many people want to set it and forget it when it comes to social media, forgetting the key word there: 'social.'

Viator settled into an easy lean against the edge of the conference table. "Does all this make sense to you?"

"Yeah, I think so."

"Good! The major thing is that if you choose to use social media, you have to remember to keep the 'social' in social media."

12 | It's All About the Click With Your Email Marketing

If you had to generate business in the next thirty days, you would always start with your current or past clients.

– Harry Wallace

"Okay, let's dig into email marketing and email newsletters."

I expressed a momentary concern. "Wait, are you talking about the junk emails I get seemingly every day about some dumb product promotion and a 10% off coupon?"

"Sort of, yes," Viator acknowledging my concern. "We all get those, but don't you have at least one or two email newsletters you always open?"

"Yeah, now that you mention it, I do."

"Okay, then you need to be one of those to your clientele." Viator tapped his marker on the table. "When do you think the first-ever email was sent? What about the first marketing email?"

I replied what I thought.

He said, "Not bad answers. What is considered the first true email was sent by Ray Tomlinson in 1971, which was essentially to himself because it was to another computer in the same room as he was. Then, on May 1, 1978, Gary Thuerk, a Digital Equipment Corp (DEC) Marketing Manager, sent out the first commercial mass email.

"Now, for better or worse, he is considered 'the father of spam,' but he likes to think of himself as 'the father of e-marketing. There's a difference.' And I tend to agree with him too. Spam is something you never signed up for or wanted in the first place, but email marketing is focused on a qualified and targeted list of people interested in you and your services—or they find your information valuable."[1, 2]

Viator went on to say, "While the list went to several hundred people, DEC ultimately sold approximately $13+ million based on the email. It would be over 98 million today if you adjusted it for inflation."

"Talk about a return on investment," I remarked, recognizing the potential value that lay within.

"Exactly! And that is just one reason marketers love email marketing so much. You can get a good bang for your buck as long as you provide value."

Viator then brought out a piece of paper from his leather laptop bag with a list of ten statistics:

1. Nearly all email users check their inbox every day, with some checking 20 times a day. Of the people who check their email daily, six out of ten checks it first thing in the morning.[3]
2. Americans average five hours each day checking email!.[4]
3. Three out of five people will often check their email before doing anything else online.[5]
4. Six out of ten Millennials (born between 1981 and 1996) primarily use their smartphone to check email.[6]
5. Over seven out of ten Baby Boomers (born between 1946 and 1964) and Gen X (born between 1965 and 1980) think email is the most personal channel to receive brand communications. This number drops slightly to six out of ten for Millennials and Gen Z.[7]
6. The average CTR for email across all industries is 10.29 percent.[8]
7. For every $1 a marketer spends on email marketing, they will typically receive $36 in return.[9]
8. Nearly eight out of ten marketers say email marketing is

in their top three marketing channels by effectiveness.[10]

9.   The average email open rate is almost 20%.[11]

10. 85% of entrepreneurs send email newsletters.[12]

"Impressive list there, don't you think?"

I nodded my head in agreement with him.

"You see, email marketing is one of the most personal and direct ways of communicating with your clients and potential clients. Therefore, the list of email addresses in your Customer Relationship Management (CRM) or email subscribers is one of the most important elements of your marketing strategy."

If I am honest, I was feeling overwhelmed by the prospect of doing an email newsletter, I couldn't help but express my uncertainty. "Well, this is all well and good, but I have never done an email newsletter before; I don't even know where I would start."

"Not a problem," he said, pushing off the table and walking to the whiteboard.

"If you have never done a newsletter, you need to warm your clients to the idea. There is a bit of an art to warming up a cold email list.

"You have to be like Adele and say hello again to see if they still want to connect with you. This is a good opportunity to go over what you have to offer and gauge whether they are still interested in the value you bring to the table. You might need to remind them how they got on the list in the first place. Once you have that done, you can use the email to your advantage."

Then he wrote these items down:

1. Getting Your Email Delivered
2. Getting Your Email Opened
3. Write like a Human and to One Person
4. Consistency is key
5. Always be sharing Value
6. Focus on Building Relationships
7. Never Buy a List
8. Keep Mobile in Mind
9. Focus on Your CTA Buttons
10. It's All About the Click
11. Include Videos to Boost Clicks

1. Getting Your Email Delivered
2. Getting Your Email Opened
3. Write Like a Human and to One Person
4. Consistency is Key
5. Always Be Sharing Value
6. Focus on Building Relationships
7. Never Buy a List
8. Keep Mobile in Mind
9. Focus on Your CTA Buttons
10. It's All About the Click
11. Include Videos to Boost Clicks

"Okay, let's look at each one of those."

GETTING YOUR EMAIL DELIVERED

Three things to help get your email delivered:

1. You don't want to use your free personal email to send an email newsletter. While you can send emails to around 100 people at a time, you are limited in the number you can send in a day.
2. To ensure your emails get delivered, you have to use a commercial email marketing platform. This not only gets you past the 100 emails at a time issue, but it also helps you to avoid ending up in the spam folder.
3. Stay clear of spammy phrases and resist the temptation to clutter your emails with too many images or links.

GETTING YOUR EMAIL OPENED: PIQUE THEIR CURIOSITY

Crafting a compelling subject line is vital if you want to increase the chances of your email getting opened. It's essential to keep in mind that your email will likely be competing for attention among countless others in your prospect's inbox. Therefore, your subject line needs to pique their curiosity and inspire them to click on your email.

WRITE LIKE A HUMAN AND TO ONE PERSON

Ensure you are writing it like a human and writing it to one person. Email is personal; the more personal you can make it feel, the better your emails will do.

CONSISTENCY IS KEY

Also, like with your blogs, consistency is key. At the end of the day, your email marketing campaign is a touchpoint for brand recognition. Therefore, if you only send an email every few months or when some event is happening, people will forget they were subscribed and wonder who you are. Even worse, if you email your list too often, they may think you are like that stage-five clinger ex they had; no one wants to go through that again.

ALWAYS BE SHARING VALUE

If you are just emailing, then you're wasting your time and your subscribers' time. All healthy relationships are built on a value exchange. Therefore, don't let all your emails be pure sales pitches or dumb product promotions.

FOCUS ON BUILDING RELATIONSHIPS

Like what you do with your day-to-day business, email marketing is about building relationships. Use email marketing to help you with that. Don't get caught up in the number of subscribers but think about whether those are truly engaged with you and getting value out of what you are sending.

NEVER BUY A LIST

Avoid purchasing, renting, swapping, or borrowing lists. Seriously, just don't do it. There's no good reason to go down that path. These shenanigans can hurt your brand, mess up your email deliverability, and even get your email tossed into the dreaded spam folder.

KEEP MOBILE IN MIND

On average, eight out of ten people will read your email on a mobile device. Therefore, the design of your email matters. Make sure it looks good on both a mobile device and a desktop.

FOCUS ON YOUR CTA BUTTONS

Most people will scan or skim their email more than on the web. This is why having a clear call-to-action (CTA) button that even the fastest email skimmers can see is critical.

Look at your views, and if most of your opens are on mobile, you might want a CTA to go all the way across the page, so it's easy to click with either hand. But if most are on the desktop, then aligning the button on the left might be better.

IT'S ALL ABOUT THE CLICK

Emails aren't the end-all, be-all of the sales process; they are just one step in it. The goal of an email should be to inform, educate, and prompt the reader to click on through to your site, where you have more of a chance to convert that click.

INCLUDE VIDEOS TO BOOST CLICKS

Emails with videos generally have a click-through rate (CTR) that's 52% higher than emails containing just images.

"I think I'm beginning to understand more now," I said. "Email marketing is just like everything else: a tool I can use to drive traffic back to my website where, if it's done right, it is set up to convert."

"I couldn't have said it better myself," Viator said with a grin.

13 | Everyone Has a Story, Use Video to Tell It

Every person has a story, every business has a story, and prospects and customers love good stories. People connect with stories that are personal, telling, truthful, and relevant.

— John Jantsch

"Let's talk about videos now," Viator said. "What are your initial thoughts on it as a marketing tool?"

I told him my thoughts on the entire subject.

He said, "When I bring up video to most of my clients, I'm hit with a healthy dose of skepticism and pushback. They will say something like:

- It seems like a lot of work.
- I don't want to be on camera.
- It will be too expensive.
- I don't have time to do videos.

"I understand the skepticism, but video can be a potent marketing tool. It can help a rural business reach a wider audience and build stronger connections with your community.

"With the increase in access to broadband internet, video has become a popular way for businesses of all sizes and places to engage with prospects and clients to capture their attention. Companies everywhere are jumping on the video bandwagon in hopes of gaining a few more eyeballs. Still with me?"

"Yeah."

"Great," he said. "Why do you think videos are so effective?"

> - Easy for people to consume
> - Communicates a lot of information in a short time
> - Easy to watch on various devieces

I thought for a moment, but Viator didn't give me the chance to respond. "I will tell you why," he said, proceeding to erase what he had before and write on the whiteboard.

- Easy for viewers to consume
- Ability to communicate a lot of information in a short amount of time
- Easy to watch on various devices (mobile, tablet, desktop, or TV)

He went on to say, "The reason video is so easy to consume is because it is multi-sensory. By combining moving images, sound, and music, you can capture the viewer's attention and keep them engaged. Speaking of engagement, if someone is busy, a video might be faster for them. Reading requires a certain level of attention and focus, whereas a video can be watched passively on a variety of devices.

"Something else I want you to think about is video can also help improve your SEO."

My ears perked up. "Really, how so?"

"That is an easy answer; you see, by putting a video on your page, you can increase the quality of the page because it's another way to consume the information, increasing the time the user stays on the page. This is called dwell time; best we can tell, it's a factor.

"Think about this: if you have a video, you can take the script you wrote and make it into a blog post. Then you have two ways to consume the information: they can watch it or read it.

"Now, there are lots of other ways to use video. For example, you could:

- Break it down into separate videos
- Take the script and turn it into a blog post
- Have it transcribed for closed captions
- Shorten and crop it for social media
- Pull the audio and turn it into a podcast

"The list goes on and on," he exclaimed, emphasizing the array of possibilities.

"I see your point," I acknowledged.

"Good. Now let's talk about the overall types of videos you might want to create, what to do with them, and how you can incorporate them into your overall marketing strategy. If you start on video, you might be tempted to try to do funny videos, but the thing is, you need to start with the ones that will help you get the most bang for your buck."

He turned and wrote these on the board:

- Education
- Engagement
- Emotion
- Empathy

- Education

- Engagement

- Emotion

- Empathy

EDUCATION

"Okay, let's start with education. These videos will help prospects digest information and remember what they've learned. Examples may include a demo of you or someone else showing a product you use or how to do something, also known as 'how-to' or 'explainer' videos. It could be you sharing knowledge and expertise around an upcoming change in the industry or your thoughts on new legislation affecting your industry and what it means for your prospect or client. Testimonial videos would also fall under this category. If you can get a client to come on and talk about your services, those are pure gold!"

ENGAGEMENT

"An engagement video captures the audience's attention and encourages interaction. They can be entertaining, interactive, or thought-provoking. For a rural small business, these can spark conversations, gather feedback, or generate buzz around your services or something you are considering offering. They can also be a behind-the-scenes or a day-in-the-life type video.

EMOTION AND EMPATHY

"Emotionally-driven videos aim to evoke strong feelings and create a connection with prospects by telling stories or highlighting meaningful experiences. An emotional-style video can help humanize your business and forge an emotional bond with prospects and clients.

Empathy-based videos go hand in hand with emotional ones. They differ because they will focus on understanding and relating to the viewer's emotions and experiences, showing your care for your client's needs and challenges.

These can include real-life stories, testimonials, or interviews that highlight how you and your business have positively impacted people's lives.

"The bottom line is that video is an incredibly powerful marketing tool to help you reach a wider audience and build stronger connections within your community."

14 | Bringing It All Together

"There is one final thing I want to talk about: being involved in your community," Viator said his voice brimming with passion.

"What do you mean by community?" I asked.

"Okay, think about this; according to the Pew Research Center, four out of ten rural residents say they know all or most of their neighbors, and six out of ten of us have lived in a rural area for more than 11 years. The University of Minnesota Rural Health Research Center says that nearly three out of ten of us will drive more than 30 minutes to work."

"That is great and all, but what is your point?"

"Like I said at the start of our journey, unless you live in a rural area, you don't get it.

"We typically have a slower pace of life, which may or may not be a good thing. Farm equipment or animals tend to be what causes a traffic jam versus the gridlock you see in suburban and urban areas. We also have a closer connection with neighbors through our churches, civic organizations, business networking groups, and the local Chamber of Commerce.

"We also know that sometimes in a rural area, it's not always what you know, but who you know, or who knows you.

"Bob Hoffman said something to the effect that it doesn't matter the size of your business or where you are at; the most important thing is that you have to become famous. In other words, you have to become an influencer in your area. Now, this could be in your industry, your geographic area, or both," Viator said.

"I get what you're saying, but isn't that what we have digital marketing for?" I asked.

"Yes," he said, "but even in a rural area, you still have to get out and be seen. As you build your name and reputation, people will still need to find you, and that is where the digital marketing part comes in."

Viator looked at me inquisitively and said, "What do you think? Do you think that everything I have shown you will help your business succeed?"

"Yeah, I think so," I said confidently.

"Great. I want to show you one last thing." Viator called up a car, and we headed back to where it all began: the road where I first met him.

Viator said, "If you recall, I told you I would show you where the big main road went and that you didn't want to go down it, correct?"

"Yeah."

"Follow me, and I will show you where that road leads."

We walked a narrow, winding path and eventually came to an overlook from which I could see everything. Viator pointed out all the areas and places we had been, and then he pointed out the main road.

"Follow it from where I first met you, and you will see why I said not to go that way" pointing out toward the horizon as he said it.

As I started tracing the road, it got bigger and wider and full of big-name companies. Eventually, it came to what looked like a toll booth. The big companies were passing through, but the smaller ones were stopped. "I don't understand. Why can't the little companies go through?"

"You see, the big companies' marketing and advertising is different from yours. They can do more mass marketing. They can throw money at everything that comes down the line. So essentially, what they are doing is shotgunning everything. But with you, you need more of a rifle approach, so it is much more targeted. I knew when I met you that if you followed the big boys down the road, you wouldn't be able to make it."

We stood silently for a few moments, then Viator started back down and motioned for me to follow.

When we got back down, Otto, Constanze, and Phoebus stood at the crossroads. They looked at me and then looked at Viator. You could cut the tension between them with a knife.

Breaking the stillness, Constanze locked eyes with me and uttered her cutting remark, "Well, it looks like Viator has done a number on you."

Confusion etched across my face, I couldn't help but question their accusations. "What do you mean?" I inquired, my voice tinged with defiance.

Otto interjected with a mocking tone, "You have bought into his lies hook, line, and sinker, even though you know how hard it will be to do what he has taught you."

Constanze added fuel to the fire, emphasizing the challenges that lay ahead. "Think about all the effort you will have to put in to change and do all that. You were already working yourself to the bone. How are you going to add this to your plate?"

Phoebus joined in, his words laced with fear and doubt, "Aren't you afraid of what will happen if you follow what he has told you and it still fails?"

I thought for a moment, then crossed my arms. "I hear what you're saying, but I don't think it will be as bad as you say it will be. I think you want to see me fail."

Their collective gasp filled the air, and their unified gaze conveyed both shock and disdain. In unison they said, "Well, don't come crying back to us when what he told you leads to failure."

They all gasped, looked at me in unison, and said, "Well, don't come crying back to us when what he told you leads to failure."

And like magic, they were gone.

I looked at Viator and said, "What just happened?"

Viator's eyes gleamed with satisfaction as he spoke, "You completed the final task."

Perplexed, I pressed further, "What task? What do you mean?"

Viator's voice carried a hint of triumph as he spoke, "You see, you asked me for help, and you now see that what you did wasn't the best method. You were also vulnerable, open-minded, growth-oriented. And more importantly, you trusted me, you believed in yourself, and you believed in the process. By doing that, you overcame your own fear and need to maintain the status quo. You truly realize now what you need to do to make your business successful."

"What now, then?" I inquired, my voice filled with anticipation.

Viator said, "What do you want to do?"

Confusion tinged my response, "What do you mean? I want to grow the business and use what you showed me to do that!"

"And to do that, what must you do?" Viator questioned.

"Well, I still have to get back home," I said frustratedly.

"Do you remember what step one was?"

I thought momentarily, then it hit me, "Ask!" I said enthusiastically and proudly.

Viator grinned. "That's it."

Then magically, a door appeared.

Viator said, "This door will lead back to the real world, not the world that exists here."

Uncertainty crept into my voice as I interjected, "Wait, how will I find you when I get back if I need help?"

Confidently, Viator handed me a business card belonging to a trusted friend. "I don't think you will need any help, but if you do, they can help you. Just shoot them an email when if and when you need them."

With that, I waved goodbye to Viator and stepped through the door.

The next thing I knew, I was in a hospital bed, but I remembered everything about my journey in that other world.

A nurse came into the room and started checking my vitals. When she noticed I had come to, she said, "Welcome back."

"Welcome back?" I questioned.

Did she know where I had been? Was it real or a dream?

"I mean, welcome back to the conscious world. You were in a bad wreck and have been in a coma for the past several days."

I couldn't believe what I was hearing. My mind was racing, and I was filled with questions. Was meeting Viator a dream?

I asked the nurse for a notepad and pen and started to jot down things I remembered Viator had told me.

After another day, I was cleared to go home. As I was checking out, the nurse brought my personal effects. I dumped everything out on the bed, and in a folder were all the pieces of paper and notes I had taken with Viator. But how?

Now I had to find that card! I fumbled around through everything and found it. I emailed the address on the card with shaky hands and waited for a reply. Luckily, I got an email back before I left the hospital.

A few emails and days later, I was in my local coffee shop waiting to meet up with the guy who I had emailed back and forth with. As I kept a keen eye on the door, a man walked in that looked an awful lot like Viator.

He walked over to me and said, "I see you made it back safe and sound."

He even sounded like Viator.

"Wait a minute. You are Viator, aren't you?" I said with excitement and inquisitively.

He laughed, winked at me, and said, "They call me Chad around here. But let's grab a coffee and talk about helping you grow the business."

Key Takeaways and Notes

Now that you have finished reading this book, are you ready for the most exciting offer of your life? Hold onto your bookmarks because I've got a deal that'll blow your literary socks off!

Introducing the one and only super-duper, life-changing "Key Takeaways and Notes!" That's right, you just finished this incredible journey, but you know what's even more amazing? Tapping into "your notes" all in this exclusive download!

But wait, there's more!

With our "Key Takeaways and Notes," you won't just be smarter; you'll also get "Viator's Whiteboard Scribbling and Handouts."

But hold on, folks, that's not all!

Scan the QR Code, fill out the short form, and I will throw in a bonus! "Book a free call with Chad." Yes, you read that right! I am giving away a free consultation just for you!

So why wait?

Don't miss out on this extraordinary offer of a lifetime! Scan the QR Code below to get your download and get ready to transform your rural small business like never before.

Endnotes

CHAPTER 1

1. Wickman, Gino. *Traction: Get A Grip on Your Business*, 24. Perseus Distribution Services, 2012.

2. McIntyre, Georgia. "What Percentage of Small Businesses Fail?" *Fundera*, Last modified November 20, 2020. Accessed May 1, 2023. https://www.fundera.com/blog/what-percentage-of-small-businesses-fail.

3. Johnson, Cameron. "Looking Back on the Origin of Skip Intro Five Years Later." *About Netflix*. Last modified March 17, 2022. Accessed April 6, 2023. https://about.netflix.com/en/news/looking-back-on-the-origin-of-skip-intro-five-years-later.

4. Vaile, Ronald S. "Harvard Business Review 1927-04: Vol 5 ISS 3 : Free Download, Borrow, and Streaming." *Internet Archive*. Harvard Business Review, April 1, 1927. Last modified April 1, 1927. Accessed April 6, 2023. https://archive.org/details/sim_harvard-business-review_1927-04_5_3.

5. Van den Brink, Koen. "The Importance of Investing in Marketing During a Recession." *TNA Suite*. Last modified April 30, 2020. Accessed April 22, 2023. https://www.tnasuite.com/blog/the-importance-of-investing-in-marketing-during-a-recession/.

6. Sinek, Simon. *Start with Why: How Great Leaders Inspire Everyone to Take Action*, 10. New York, NY: Portfolio/Penguin, 2009.

7. Sinek, Simon. *Start with Why: How Great Leaders Inspire Everyone to Take Action*, 105–106. New York, NY: Portfolio/Penguin, 2009.

CHAPTER 2

1. Rauschuber, Catherine. "Yellow Pages Ordinance Proposed by Supervisor David Chiu." https://sfenvironment.org/sites/default/files/editor-uploads/zero_waste/pdf/sfe_zw_yellow_pages_legislation_faq.pdf

2. Virgin, Bill. "The Internet Hasn't Been Able to Replace the ... - Tacoma News Tribune." Here's One Thing the Internet Hasn't Replaced Adequately: the Paper Phone Directory. *Tacoma News Tribune* , August 8, 2020. Last modified August 8, 2020. Accessed June 8, 2022. https://www.thenewstribune.com/news/business/biz-columns-blogs/article244779037.html.

3. Kitson, Harry Dexter. *The Mind of the Buyer: A Psychology of Selling*, 29–30. New York, 1923.

4. Ries, Al, and Jack Trout. *The 22 Immutable Laws of Marketing: Violate Them at Your Own Risk*, 125–125. New York, NY: HarperBusiness, 1994.

5. Blick, Dee. *The Ultimate Small Business Marketing Book*, 20. Croydon: Filament publishing, 2011.

6. Dib, Allan. *1-Page Marketing Plan: Get New Customers, Make More Money, And Stand Out From The Crowd*, 15–16. Pgw, 2021.

CHAPTER 3

1. Hoffman, Bob. *Advertising for Skeptics*, 16–17. Las Vegas, NV: Type A Group, 2020.

2. Hoffman, Bob. *Advertising for Skeptics*, 13. Las Vegas, NV: Type A Group, 2020.

3. Hoffman, Bob. *Advertising for Skeptics*, 14. Las Vegas, NV: Type A Group, 2020.

4. Hoffman, Bob. *Adscam: How Online Advertising Gave Birth to One of History's Greatest Frauds, and Became a Threat to Democracy*, 35–35. Oakland, CA: Type A Group, 2022.

5. Hoffman, Bob. *Adscam: How Online Advertising Gave Birth to One of History's Greatest Frauds, and Became a Threat to Democracy*, 35–39. Oakland, CA: Type A Group, 2022.

6. Hoffman, Bob. *Adscam: How Online Advertising Gave Birth to One of History's Greatest Frauds, and Became a Threat to Democracy*, 78. Oakland, CA: Type A Group, 2022.

7. Hoffman, Bob. *Adscam: How Online Advertising Gave Birth to One of History's Greatest Frauds, and Became a Threat to Democracy*, 59-60. Oakland, CA: Type A Group, 2022.

8. Hoffman, Bob. *Advertising for Skeptics*, 19-20. Las Vegas, NV: Type A Group, 2020.

9. Hoffman, Bob. *Advertising for Skeptics*, 19-20. Las Vegas, NV: Type A Group, 2020.

10. Birnbaum, Emily. "Group Backed by Tech Giants Claims Thousands of Members. Many Have Never Heard of It." *POLITICO*. Last modified March 30, 2022. Accessed April 13, 2023. https://www.politico.com/news/2022/03/30/connected-commerce-council-amazon-google-lobbying-00021801.

CHAPTER 5

1. Halligan, Brian, and Dharmesh Shah. *Inbound Marketing: Attract, Engage, and Delight Customers Online*, 110. Wiley, 2015.

2. Blanks, Karl, Ben Jesson, and Avinash Kaushik. *In Making Websites Win: Apply the Customer-Centric Methodology That Has Doubled the Sales of Many Leading Websites*, 30. New York, NY: Conversion Rate Experts, 2017.

3. Ogilvy, David. *Ogilvy on Advertising*, 88–90. New York, NY: Vintage Books, 1985.

4. Ogilvy, David. *Ogilvy on Advertising*, 96. New York, NY: Vintage Books, 1985.

5. Ogilvy, David. *Ogilvy on Advertising*, 97-101. New York, NY: Vintage Books, 1985.

6. Ogilvy, David. *Ogilvy on Advertising*, 96. New York, NY: Vintage Books, 1985.

7. Ogilvy, David. *Ogilvy on Advertising*, 96. New York, NY: Vintage Books, 1985.

8. Ogilvy, David. *Ogilvy on Advertising*, 96. New York, NY: Vintage Books, 1985.

9. Ogilvy, David. *Ogilvy on Advertising*, 97. New York, NY: Vintage Books, 1985.

10. Blanks, Karl, Ben Jesson, and Avinash Kaushik. *Making Websites Win: Apply the Customer-Centric Methodology That Has Doubled the Sales of Many Leading Websites*, 255. New York, NY: Conversion Rate Experts, 2017.

11. Ogilvy, David. Ogilvy on Advertising, 97. New York, NY: Vintage Books, 1985.

12. Blanks, Karl, Ben Jesson, and Avinash Kaushik. *Making Websites Win: Apply the Customer-Centric Methodology That Has Doubled the Sales of Many Leading Websites*, 255. New York, NY: Conversion Rate Experts, 2017.

13. Bailey, Craig. "Content Is King by Bill Gates." Content Is King By Bill Gates. Last modified May 31, 2010. Accessed April 13, 2023. https://www.craigbailey.net/content-is-king-by-bill-gates/.

14. Blanks, Karl, Ben Jesson, and Avinash Kaushik. *Making Websites Win: Apply the Customer-Centric Methodology That Has Doubled the Sales of Many Leading Websites*, 161. New York, NY: Conversion Rate Experts, 2017.

15. "Internet/Broadband Fact Sheet." Internet/Broadband Fact Sheet. Pew Research Center, April 7, 2021. Last modified April 7, 2021. Accessed April 13, 2023. https://www.pewresearch.org/internet/fact-sheet/internet-broadband/.

16. "Internet/Broadband Fact Sheet." *Internet/Broadband Fact Sheet. Pew Research Center*, April 7, 2021. Last modified April 7, 2021. Accessed April 13, 2023. https://www.pewresearch.org/internet/fact-sheet/internet-broadband/.

17. "Internet/Broadband Fact Sheet." *Internet/Broadband Fact Sheet. Pew Research Center*, April 7, 2021. Last modified April 7, 2021. Accessed April 13, 2023. https://www.pewresearch.org/internet/fact-sheet/internet-broadband/.

18. Miller, Donald, and J. J. Peterson. *Marketing Made Simple: A Step-by-Step Storybrand Guide for Any Business*, 57–67. New York, NY: Harpercollins Leadership, 2021.

19. Leaning, Brittany. "48 Call-to-Action Examples You Can't Help but Click." 48 Call-to-Action Examples You Can't Help But Click. *HubSpot*, December 29, 2022. Last modified December 29, 2022. Accessed April 13, 2023. https://blog.hubspot.com/marketing/call-to-action-examples.

20. Gonzalez, Oscar. "Where to Put the Primary Button?" *Medium - UX Collective*, December 7, 2022. Last modified December 7, 2022. Accessed April 19, 2023. https://uxdesign.cc/where-to-put-the-primary-button-5bd8cb1764c4.

21. Poza, Diego. "7 Simple Hacks to Supercharge Your Registration Process." 7 Simple Hacks To Supercharge Your Registration Process. Auth0, April 19, 2016. Last modified April 19, 2016. Accessed April 13, 2023. https://auth0.com/blog/supercharge-your-registration-process/.

22. Cialdini, Robert B. *Influence, New and Expanded: The Psychology of Persuasion*, 314–315. New York, NY: Harper Business, 2021.

23. Halligan, Brian, and Dharmesh Shah. *Inbound Marketing: Attract, Engage, and Delight Customers Online*, 113. Wiley, 2015.

CHAPTER 6

1. Lyons, Kelly. What Are E-A-T and YMYL in Seo & How to Optimize for Them. Semrush, November 30, 2022. Last modified November 30, 2022. Accessed April 13, 2023. https://www.semrush.com/blog/eat-and-ymyl-new-google-search-guidelines-acronyms-of-quality-content/.

2. "Our Latest Update to the Quality Rater Guidelines: E-A-T Gets an Extra E for Experience." Google Search Central. Google, December 15, 2022. Last modified December 15, 2022. Accessed April 13, 2023. https://developers.google.com/search/blog/2022/12/google-raters-guidelines-e-e-a-t.

3. Ray, Lily. "E-E-A-T And Major Updates to Google's Quality Rater Guidelines." Search Engine Land. Last modified December 15, 2022. Accessed April 13, 2023. https://searchengineland.com/google-search-quality-rater-guidelines-changes-december-2022-390350.

4. "Our Latest Update to the Quality Rater Guidelines: E-A-T Gets an Extra E for Experience." Google Search Central Blog. Google, December 15, 2022. Last modified December 15, 2022. Accessed April 13, 2023. https://developers.google.com/search/blog/2022/12/google-raters-guidelines-e-e-a-t.

5. Scott, David Meerman. *The New Rules of Marketing and PR: How to Use Content Marketing, Podcasting, Social Media, AI, Live Video, and Newsjacking to Reach Buyers Directly*, 90–91. Hoboken, NJ: John Wiley & Sons, Inc., 2022.

6. Lincoln, John E. "The SEO and User Science Behind Long-Form Content." Search Engine Land. Last modified September 28, 2015. Accessed April 13, 2023. https://searchengineland.com/seo-user-science-behind-long-form-content-230721.

7. Sukhraj, Ramona. "28 Little-Known Blogging Statistics to Help Shape Your Strategy in 2019." IMPACT Inbound Marketing Agency. Last modified January 17, 2017. Accessed April 13, 2023. https://www.impactplus.com/blog/blogging-statistics-to-boost-your-strategy.

8. Ouellette, Coral. "Ultimate List of Blogging Statistics and Facts (Updated for 2023)." OptinMonster. Last modified April 22, 2022. Accessed April 13, 2023. https://optinmonster.com/blogging-statistics/.

9.   Bump, Pamela. "31 Business Blogging Stats You Need to Know in 2021." HubSpot Blog. HubSpot, May 11, 2020. Last modified May 11, 2020. Accessed April 13, 2023. https://blog.hubspot.com/marketing/business-blogging-in-2015.

10.   Ouellette, Coral. "Ultimate List of Blogging Statistics and Facts (Updated for 2023)." OptinMonster. Last modified April 22, 2022. Accessed April 13, 2023. https://optinmonster.com/blogging-statistics/.

11.   Balkhi, Syed. "4 Reasons Your Website Conversions Are Low (and How to Fix Them)." Constant Contact. Last modified September 8, 2020. Accessed April 13, 2023. https://www.constantcontact.com/blog/website-conversions/.

12.   "30 Digital Marketing Statistics You Shouldn't Miss." Optimind Technology Solutions. Last modified March 10, 2022. Accessed April 13, 2023. https://www.myoptimind.com/30-digital-marketing-statistics-you-shouldnt-miss/.

13.   McCraw, Austin. "This Just Tested: Stock Images or Real People?" MarketingExperiments. Last modified May 8, 2011. Accessed April 13, 2023. https://marketingexperiments.com/digital-advertising/stock-images-tested.

14.   Shepherd, Maddie. "11 Business Blogging Statistics Marketers Need to Know." Fundera Ledger. Fundera, July 23, 2019. Last modified July 23, 2019. Accessed April 13, 2023. https://www.fundera.com/resources/business-blogging-statistics.

15.   Ouellette, Coral. "Ultimate List of Blogging Statistics and Facts (Updated for 2023)." OptinMonster. Last modified April 22, 2022. Accessed April 13, 2023. https://optinmonster.com/blogging-statistics/.

16.   Ray, Lily. "E-E-A-T And Major Updates to Google's Quality Rater Guidelines." Search Engine Land. Last modified December 15, 2022. Accessed April 13, 2023. https://searchengineland.com/google-search-quality-rater-guidelines-changes-december-2022-390350.

17.   "Search Quality Evaluator Guidelines." Accessed April 13, 2023. https://static.googleusercontent.com/media/guidelines.raterhub.com/en//searchqualityevaluatorguidelines.pdf.

18.   Hall, Kindra. *Stories That Stick: How Storytelling Can Captivate Customers, Influence Audiences, and Transform Your Business*, 66–68. HarperCollins Leadership, 2019.

19.   Hall, Kindra. In *Stories That Stick: How Storytelling Can Captivate Customers, Influence Audiences, and Transform Your Business*, 64. HarperCollins Leadership, 2019.

20.   Ries, Al, and Jack Trout. In *The 22 Immutable Laws of Marketing: Violate Them at Your Own Risk*, 42-23 New York, NY: HarperBusiness, 1994.

21.   "Content Trends: Preferences Emerge along Generational Fault Lines." Accessed April 13, 2023. https://cdn2.hubspot.net/hubfs/53/assets/hubspot.com/research/reports/HubSpot%20Content%20Trends%20-%20Generational%20Fault%20Lines.pdf?t=1511049274375.

CHAPTER 7

1. Fox, Jeffrey J. *How to Become a Rainmaker: The People Who Get and Keep Customers*, 101. London: Vermilion, 2000.

2. Fox, Jeffrey J. *How to Become a Rainmaker: The People Who Get and Keep Customers*, 101-102. London: Vermilion, 2000.

3. Sheridan, Marcus. *They Ask, You Answer Revised and Updated: A Revolutionary Approach to Inbound Sales, Content Marketing, and Today's Digital Consumer*, 108. Hoboken: Wiley, 2019.

4. "River Pools Company - 16913000 Revenue." Kona Equity. Accessed April 13, 2023. https://www.konaequity.com/company/river-pools-company-4019779750/.

5. "River Pools - Overview, News & Competitors | Zoominfo.com." Accessed April 13, 2023. https://www.zoominfo.com/c/river-pools-co/158384510.

6. Sheridan, Marcus. *They Ask, You Answer Revised and Updated: A Revolutionary Approach to Inbound Sales, Content Marketing, and Today's Digital Consumer*, 14. Hoboken: Wiley, 2019.

7. Sheridan, Marcus. *They Ask, You Answer Revised and Updated: A Revolutionary Approach to Inbound Sales, Content Marketing, and Today's Digital Consumer*, 14. Hoboken: Wiley, 2019.

8. Sheridan, Marcus. *They Ask, You Answer Revised and Updated: A Revolutionary Approach to Inbound Sales, Content Marketing, and Today's Digital Consumer*, 21. Hoboken: Wiley, 2019.

9. "5 Ways the Future of B2B Buying Will Rewrite the Rules of Effective Selling." Last modified 2020. Accessed April 13, 2023. https://emtemp.gcom.cloud/ngw/globalassets/en/sales-service/documents/trends/5-ways-the-future-of-b2b-buying.pdf?trk=public_post_comment-text.

10. Sheridan, Marcus. *They Ask, You Answer Revised and Updated: A Revolutionary Approach to Inbound Sales, Content Marketing, and Today's Digital Consumer*, 10. Hoboken: Wiley, 2019.

11. Sheridan, Marcus. *They Ask, You Answer Revised and Updated: A Revolutionary Approach to Inbound Sales, Content Marketing, and Today's Digital Consumer*, 59. Hoboken: Wiley, 2019.

12. Dixon, Matthew, and Ted McKenna. *The Jolt Effect: How High Performers Overcome Customer Indecision*, 8. New York: Portfolio/Penguin, 2022.

13. Dixon, Matthew, and Ted McKenna. *The Jolt Effect: How High Performers Overcome Customer Indecision*, 14. New York: Portfolio/Penguin, 2022.

14. Dixon, Matthew, and Ted McKenna. *The Jolt Effect: How High Performers Overcome Customer Indecision*, 13. New York: Portfolio/Penguin, 2022.

15. Dixon, Matthew, and Ted McKenna. *The Jolt Effect: How High Performers Overcome Customer Indecision*, 17. New York: Portfolio/Penguin, 2022.

CHAPTER 8

1. April 18, 2006. "Vocabulary: 'Landing Page.'" Seth's Blog. Last modified April 18, 2006. Accessed April 13, 2023. https://seths.blog/2006/04/vocabulary_land/.

2. Halligan, Brian, and Dharmesh Shah. *Inbound Marketing: Attract, Engage, and Delight Customers Online*, 109-122. Wiley, 2015.

3. "Ogilvy & Mather's House Ads: The Ultimate Swipeable Ads for Freelancers." Info Marketing Money Machines. Accessed April 13, 2023. https://infomarketingblog.com/wordpress/ogilvy-mathers-house-ads-the-ultimate-swipeable-ads-for-freelancers/.

4. Schwartz, Barry. "Pigeon: Search Engine Land's Name for the New Google Local Search Update." Search Engine Land. Last modified July 25, 2014. Accessed April 13, 2023. https://searchengineland.com/pigeon-search-engine-lands-name-new-google-local-search-update-197932.

5. Local, Mike Blumenthal in Google+. "Pigeon – an Anecdotal Impact Report." Mike Blumenthal | Developing Knowledge about Local Search. Last modified August 4, 2014. Accessed April 13, 2023. https://blumenthals.com/blog/2014/08/03/pigeon-an-anecdotal-impact-report/.

CHAPTER 9

1. Jantsch, John. *The Referral Engine: Teaching Your Business How to Market Itself*, 3. London: Portfolio, 2013.

2. Cialdini, Robert B. *Influence, New and Expanded: The Psychology of Persuasion*, 129-130. New York, NY: Harper Business, 2021.

3. Cialdini, Robert B. *Influence, New and Expanded: The Psychology of Persuasion*, 143-144. New York, NY: Harper Business, 2021.

4. Cialdini, Robert B. *Influence, New and Expanded: The Psychology of Persuasion*, 156. New York, NY: Harper Business, 2021.

5. Jantsch, John. *The Referral Engine: Teaching Your Business How to Market Itself*, 13. London: Portfolio, 2013.

6. Heath, Chip. *Making Numbers Count*, 19. Avid Reader Press / SimonSchuster, 2022.

7. Heath, Chip. *Making Numbers Count*, 19. Avid Reader Press / SimonSchuster, 2022.

8. Heath, Chip. *Making Numbers Count*, 21. Avid Reader Press / SimonSchuster, 2022.

9. Heath, Chip. *Making Numbers Count*, 22. Avid Reader Press / SimonSchuster, 2022.

10. Cialdini, Robert B. *Influence, New and Expanded: The Psychology of Persuasion*, 13-14. New York, NY: Harper Business, 2021.

11. Wintrs, Mike. "6 Tips for Spotting Fake Online Reviews during the Holiday Shopping Season." CNBC. CNBC, November 23, 2022. Last modified November 23, 2022. Accessed April 13, 2023. https://www.cnbc.com/2022/11/23/tips-for-spotting-fake-online-reviews.html.

12. Cantle, Ian, Dan Gershenson, Ray L. Perry, and Ken Tucker. *Content Marketing for Local Search: Create Content That Google Loves & Prospects Devour*, 76–79, n.d.

13. Caponi, Todd. *The Transparency Sale: How Unexpected Honesty and Understanding the Buying Brain Can Transform Your Results*, 2. United States: Ideapress Publishing, 2018.

14. Eisenberg, Daniel. "It's an Ad, AD, AD World." *Time Inc.*, August 26, 2002. Last modified August 26, 2002. Accessed April 13, 2023. https://content.time.com/time/magazine/article/0,9171,344045,00.html.

CHAPTER 11

1. Battelle, John. "John Battelle's Search Blog to Be Clear: Do Not Build Your Brand House on Land You Don't Own." John Battelle's Search Blog. Last modified February 28, 2014. Accessed April 19, 2023. https://battellemedia.com/archives/2014/02/to-be-clear-do-not-build-your-brand-house-on-land-you-dont-own.

2. "History of Facebook." Wikipedia, April 12, 2023. Last modified April 12, 2023. Accessed April 13, 2023. https://en.wikipedia.org/wiki/History_of_Facebook.

3. Rose, Robert. "Yet Another Reason Not to Build Your Content Home on Rented Land." Content Marketing Institute. Last modified April 29, 2022. Accessed April 13, 2023. https://contentmarketinginstitute.com/articles/dont-build-content-rented-land.

4. Tapper, Jake. "Bruce Schneier: . 'Don't Make the Mistake of Thinking You're Facebook's Customer, You're Not – You're the Product. Its Customers Are the Advertisers.'." Twitter. Twitter, March 21, 2018. Last modified March 21, 2018. Accessed April 13, 2023. https://twitter.com/jaketapper/status/976473447374221313.

5. "Quote Research, Author. "You're Not the Customer; You're the Product." Quote Investigator. Last modified December 30, 2020. Accessed April 13, 2023. https://quoteinvestigator.com/2017/07/16/product.

6. Television Delivers People. Television Delivers People (1973). YouTube, 2011. Accessed April 13, 2023. https://www.youtube.com/watch?v=LvZYwaQlJsg. Uploaded by: KunstSpektrum, Copyright date within video: Mar 30, 1973, (Quotation starts at 0 minute 54 seconds of 6 minutes 55 seconds) (Video of scrolling text with canned soundtrack music; Text criticizes the corporate and advertiser control of television content), (Accessed on youtube.com on May 13, 2017)

7. Scott, David Meerman. *The New Rules of Marketing and PR: How to Use Content Marketing, Podcasting, Social Media, AI, Live Video, and Newsjacking to Reach Buyers Directly*, 65-67. Hoboken: John Wiley & Sons, Inc., 2022.

8. Cialdini, Robert B. *Influence, New and Expanded: The Psychology of Persuasion*, 89-90. New York, NY: Harper Business, 2021.

9. Cialdini, Robert B. *Influence, New and Expanded: The Psychology of Persuasion*, 96-97. New York, NY: Harper Business, 2021.

10. O'Sullivan, Donie. "A Facebook Rumor about White Vans Is Spreading Fear across America | CNN Business." CNN. Cable News Network, December 5, 2019. Last modified December 5, 2019. Accessed April 13, 2023. https://www.cnn.com/2019/12/04/tech/facebook-white-vans/index.html.

11. Fedschun, Travis. "Baltimore Mayor Warns of White Van Trying to 'Snatch up Young Girls'; Police Say No Reports." Fox News. FOX News Network, December 4, 2019. Last modified December 4, 2019. Accessed April 13, 2023. https://www.foxnews.com/us/baltimore-mayor-white-van-body-part-snatch-young-girls-police-dispute.

12. Cole, Brent. *How to Win Friends and Influence People in the Digital Age*, 129. New York: Simon & Schuster Paperbacks, 2012.

13. Cole, Brent. *How to Win Friends and Influence People in the Digital Age*, 132. New York: Simon & Schuster Paperbacks, 2012.

14. Pulizzi, Joe. *Content Inc., Completely Updated and Expanded Second Edition: Start a Content-First Business, Build a Massive Audience and Become Radically Successful (with Little to No Money)*, 192. New York City: McGraw Hill, 2021.

15. Pulizzi, Joe. *Content Inc., Completely Updated and Expanded Second Edition: Start a Content-First Business, Build a Massive Audience and Become Radically Successful (with Little to No Money)*, 192-200. New York City: McGraw Hill, 2021.

16. Dib, Allan. *In The 1-Page Marketing Plan: Get New Customers, Make More Money, and Stand out from the Crowd*, 83-99. Pgw, 2021.

17. Pulizzi, Joe. *Content Inc., Completely Updated and Expanded Second Edition: Start a Content-First Business, Build a Massive Audience and Become Radically Successful (with Little to No Money)*, 151. New York City: McGraw Hill, 2021.

CHAPTER 12

1. Lee, Gary. "The Evolution of Email Marketing [Infographic]." Smart Insights. Last modified May 28, 2013. Accessed April 13, 2023. https://www.smartinsights.com/email-marketing/email-communications-strategy/email-marketing-evolution/.

2. Smith, Gina. "Unsung Innovators: Gary Thuerk, the Father of Spam." Computerworld. Computerworld, December 3, 2007. Last modified December 3, 2007. Accessed April 13, 2023. https://www.computerworld.com/article/2539767/unsung-innovators--gary-thuerk--the-father-of-spam.html.

3.   Santora, Jacinda. "Is Email Marketing Dead? Statistics Say: Not a Chance." OptinMonster. Last modified August 14, 2020. Accessed April 13, 2023. https://optinmonster.com/is-email-marketing-dead-heres-what-the-statistics-show/.

4.   Guta, Michael. "Hey Marketers, Americans Still Spend 5 Hours a Day on Email." Small Business Trends. Last modified April 16, 2021. Accessed April 13, 2023. https://smallbiztrends.com/2019/09/email-usage-statistics.html.

5.   Santora, Jacinda. "Is Email Marketing Dead? Statistics Say: Not a Chance." OptinMonster. Last modified August 14, 2020. Accessed April 13, 2023. https://optinmonster.com/is-email-marketing-dead-heres-what-the-statistics-show/.

6.   "How Millennials Actually Want Brands to Engage with Them." Bluecore. Accessed April 13, 2023. https://bluecoreweb.wpengine.com/resources/millennials-engage-brands-report-2016/.

7.   "How Millennials Actually Want Brands to Engage with Them." Bluecore. Accessed April 13, 2023. https://bluecoreweb.wpengine.com/resources/millennials-engage-brands-report-2016/.

8.   Sirohi, Aastha. "Average Email Click-through-Rate: A Guide." Constant Contact. Last modified November 1, 2022. Accessed April 13, 2023. https://www.constantcontact.com/blog/average-click-through-rate-for-email/.

9.   Moller, Megan. "The ROI of Email Marketing [Infographic]." Litmus. Last modified November 3, 2022. Accessed April 13, 2023. https://www.litmus.com/blog/infographic-the-roi-of-email-marketing/.

10.   "State of Inbound Marketing Trends - HubSpot." Accessed April 13, 2023. https://www.hubspot.com/hubfs/2022_State-of-Inbound-Marketing-Trends_71.pdf

11.   Leszczynski, Michal. "2022 Email Marketing Benchmarks." Marketing Software by GetResponse. Accessed April 13, 2023. https://www.getresponse.com/resources/reports/email-marketing-benchmarks.

12.   Pulizzi, Joe, and Brian Piper. *Epic Content Marketing, Second Edition: Break through the Clutter with a Different Story, Get the Most out of Your Content, and Build a Community in WEB3*, 71-77. McGraw-Hill Education, 2023.

Acknowledgments

If you had asked me when I graduated college if I would ever become an avid reader, I would have laughed at you. If you asked me whether I would ever write a book, I would have asked if you needed to be committed. But alas, here I am, putting the finishing touches on this. While it has been a long time coming, sometimes you just have to scratch the itch to be able to help people.

Along the way, I have been fortunate to receive support and encouragement from numerous authors, mentors, experts, friends, colleagues, and families. With immense gratitude, I extend my heartfelt thanks to each of you.

To Jared: Thanks for the support, encouragement, and telling me to "just do it."

To Barry: Thanks for telling me that I should read ten pages daily, which started this process.

To Melanie: Thanks for helping with the research portion.

To Marcus, Bob, Carrie, and Mike: Thanks for the interviews and for giving me your blessings.

To Dana: Thanks for helping with the research and edits.

To Janis, Elisabeth, and Travis: Thanks for helping with the edits; I know it was rough.

To Joe: Thanks for your advice on the design aspects. The student has become the teacher.

To Adam: Thanks for taking a chance all those years ago and supporting this itch I had to scratch.

To Stephanie, Jesse, Audrey, and Jennifer: Thanks for the conversations, editing, and marketing help. While some may think it was crazy to hire a group to help edit and market a book about marketing, I can tell you it has been well worth it!

To Mom and Dad: Thanks for all the love and support over the years.

A special thanks to the authors who wrote the books I have quoted.

And last, but certainly not least, to Amber and Raylan: I owe an immense debt of gratitude to you both.

About Chad

Chad J. Treadway knows the importance of digital marketing and is committed to helping small businesses not just embrace its benefits but break free from overwhelm and take the next right steps to leverage it for their efforts. As the Chief Smarketing Officer and Partner at Cube Creative Design in North Carolina, he helps clients survey their business needs and find customized solutions. With experience spanning advertising, marketing, design, and business development, Chad's skill set paired with his commitment to building strong client relationships helps him deliver impactful and innovative digital marketing solutions that drive growth. He draws on his small town roots and work ethic to provide thoughtful guidance tailored to each client. Chad is actively involved with the local Chambers of Commerce and business organizations in his area. He lives in North Wilkesboro with his wife Amber and son Raylan. Digital Marketing for Rural Small Businesses: A Comprehensive Guide to Getting Found on the Internet is his first published book.